A Child
Through Time

The Book of Children's History

Illustrated by Steve Noon
Written by Philip Wilkinson

Senior editor Sam Priddy
Senior art editor Fiona Macdonald
Project editor Allison Singer
Editorial assistants Sarah Foakes, Kathleen Teece
Design assistants Rhea Gaughan, Molly Lattin,
Bettina Myklebust Stovne
Additional editing by Deborah Lock,
Ruth O'Rourke-Jones, Elizabeth Yeates
Jacket co-ordinator Francesca Young
Pre-production producer Nadine King
Producer Isabell Schart
Managing editor Laura Gilbert
Managing art editor Diane Peyton Jones
Art director Martin Wilson
Publisher Sarah Larter
Publishing director Sophie Mitchell

First published in Great Britain in 2017 by
Dorling Kindersley Limited
80 Strand, London WC2R 0RL

Copyright © 2017 Dorling Kindersley Limited
A Penguin Random House Company
10 9 8 7 6 5 4 3
009–192633–Nov/2017

A CIP catalogue record for this book is
available from the British Library.
ISBN: 978-0-2412-2784-8

Printed in Dubai.

A WORLD OF IDEAS:
SEE ALL THERE IS TO KNOW

www.dk.com

Things to spot

Real life

When you see this symbol
on a page it means the
child was a real person.

See if you can find
the pigeon hidden
in each scene!

Contents

Early civilizations

Classical age

Medieval period

The experts

James Dilley   Archaeologist and European prehistory
expert at the University of Southampton, UK

Andrew Robinson   Indus Valley expert and author of
more than 25 books covering the arts and sciences

Angela McDonald   Egyptologist at the
University of Glasgow, UK

Eleanor Robson   Ancient Babylon expert
at University College London, UK

Early modern period

Modern period

Zahra Newby Ancient Greece and Rome expert at the University of Warwick, UK

David Sneath Mongol and Hun expert at the University of Cambridge, UK

Diane Davies Maya archaeologist and Honorary Research Associate at University College London, UK

Aysu Dincer Hadjianastasis Medieval expert at the University of Warwick, UK

Caroline Dodds Pennock Aztec expert at the University of Sheffield, UK

Penny Roberts Early modern expert at the University of Warwick, UK

Ed Fox Pirate expert and author, formerly the curator of the Golden Hind Museum, UK

Sarah Richardson Modern historian at the University of Warwick, UK

Early civilizations

CHAPTER ONE

Many people hunted wild animals and gathered plants for food during this period, which stretched from the earliest times to about 800 BCE. However, in some places people settled down, built the first towns and cities, started farming, and learned how to make things out of metal. Most children did chores, or helped to find or grow food.

Taya

CHILD LIVING DURING THE LAST ICE AGE

Taya is a ten-year-old girl living on the plains of Ukraine about 15,000 years ago. The weather is cold and windy, especially in winter, so Taya and her family make thick clothes of deer or mammoth hide and build strong shelters. Taya helps her mother to cook food, make tools, and prepare animal skins.

Mammoth-bone hut

Mammoth bones lock together to make a strong framework for the huts. Taya and her family cover the bones with animal skins to keep out the wind while also keeping the warmth in.

Woolly neighbours

Mammoths are the size of African elephants. They are difficult and dangerous to hunt, but the rewards are worth it. Taya's family skin them and gather their bones and tusks to make houses or tools.

▼ Village life

People in the Ice Age make everything themselves, and children play their part in all aspects of daily life. Boys and girls hunt, cook, and gather firewood.

Woman scraping animal skin on a wooden frame

Hunting party returning home

Putting meat on a skewer to cook

Herd of mammoths

Digging up roots

Dogs with a bone

Making a fire

110,000 years ago
Temperatures drop as another ice age begins.

24000 BCE
Central European sculptors make figures using baked clay.

20000 BCE
The ice age reaches its height.

15300 BCE
Artists produce cave paintings at Lascaux, France.

Red ochre powder used for cave painting

13000 BCE
People live in mammoth-bone huts at Mezhirich, Ukraine.

Braided hair

Bone necklace

Deer-skin jacket

Firewood

HOW DO WE KNOW?

People learned of the Ice Age village at Mezhirich in central Ukraine, eastern Europe, in 1965. A farmer found the remains of four mammoth-bone huts. Other finds include a painted mammoth skull that may have been used as a drum.

Mezhirich ●

Mezhirich in present-day Europe

Scraper

Flint blade

Antler hammer

Stone tools

Villagers make stone tools by hitting lumps of flint with a hammer so thin pieces break off. They then chip away at the flint pieces to make sharp blades, for cutting meat and wood, and scrapers, for cleaning animal skins.

Animal skins cover the hut's bone framework.

Decorating the house entrance

People dancing to drum music

Woman and girl sewing skins

Painting mammoth skull

Buckskin shoes stuffed with straw

12500 BCE
Settled villages with some farming spring up in the eastern Mediterranean.

10000 BCE
Rising temperatures end the ice age.

1650 BCE
Last surviving mammoths die. Species is extinct.

Mammoth tusk fossil

7

Amala

CHILD LIVING IN THE INDUS VALLEY

Amala, aged ten, lives in Mohenjo-Daro, a bustling city on the banks of the Indus River, in 2000 BCE. Her house is near the market, where her parents run a baker's shop – her father bakes bread, and Amala and her mother sell it. Their shop has local customers, including potters, jewellers, and metalworkers. Traders who travel to the city by boat come to the shop, too.

Pottery whistle that makes a sound like a bird when blown

Beaded necklace

Decorated clay pot

Cotton dress

▼ City streets

Mohenjo-Daro is a carefully planned riverside city with straight streets of mud-brick houses. Amala's house has its own water supply, but there are also public wells. There is even a system of drains to keep the city clean.

Trade

The traders who buy bread at the family's shop bring goods such as gold and copper from Arabia. These goods are weighed at the market using cube-shaped stone weights.

Stall selling fruit and vegetables

Boat on the Indus River

Hungry goat

Girl pulling wheeled toy

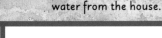
The covered drain takes waste water from the house.

c.7000 BCE
Neolithic (New Stone Age) culture is present in the Indus Valley.

c.5500 BCE
People in the region begin to produce pottery.

Terracotta figure from the Indus Valley

c.3300 BCE
Bronze working begins in the Indus Valley.

Indus cities

The Indus Valley people live in cities like Mohenjo-Daro on or near the banks of the Indus River. This area covers part of what is now India, Pakistan, and Afghanistan.

Key

Indus Valley civilization

Gold earring

Necklace of polished stone beads

Jewellery

Amala's mother has a few necklaces made of polished stones such as agate or carnelian. Women in rich families often have gold jewellery, some of which is worked into detailed designs.

Leaving a mark

The traders use stone seals bearing different images to identify their goods. Pressing the seal into a piece of clay makes a mark. When the clay dries and hardens, the trader can use it as a label.

Many seals have a distinctive picture.

Stone seal

Impression made by seal

Painting a pot

Man carrying goods in a sack

Men playing a boardgame

Citadel walls

The houses have small windows to keep them cool.

Farmer with ox and cart

Public well

Scales for weighing goods

c.2600 BCE
Indus Valley settlements grow into large cities.

The Indus city of Mohenjo-Daro from above

c.2200 BCE
Lots of traders from cities outside the Indus Valley begin to arrive.

c.1900 BCE
Indus Valley civilization begins to go into decline.

c.1700 BCE
Most of the cites are abandoned, perhaps because of drought.

Toys through time

A JOURNEY THROUGH THE HISTORY OF PLAYTIME

The earliest toys were simple, such as dolls or animals carved out of wood or counters for games made from pieces of bone. Many of today's toys, such as balls or dice, have hardly changed. However, in the 20th century motorized and computerized toys appeared, quickly becoming popular with children all over the world.

Roman dice game, called *tesserae*

Ancient Egypt

These ancient toy balls are made of linen and strips of reed. They were painted in bright colours to appeal to children. Inside are small stones that rattled around as the child rolled the ball.

Ancient Rome

Roman children played with a wide range of toys, from dolls to marbles. Games with dice and counters were enjoyed by both children and adults.

Vikings

This simple wooden horse belonged to a Norwegian Viking child in the 10th century. It is likely it was made for its owner by their father or another male relative.

Some ancient animal figures have wooden wheels.

An early rival to the teddy bear, the Billy Possum, failed to catch on.

Mid-20th century

Space was all over the news in the mid-20th century. American and Russian rocket launches led up to the first humans landing on the Moon in 1969. Space travel caught children's imaginations, and toy spacecraft and astronaut's helmets were hugely popular.

Early 20th century

The bear was developed as a soft toy in Germany and the USA at the start of the 20th century. It was named the "teddy bear" after US President Theodore Roosevelt around 1902. Teddies were soon a favourite with children in the USA and across Europe, too.

19th century

Children have played with dolls for thousands of years. They were popular girls' toys in the 19th century, when they often had porcelain heads and bodies and were finely dressed in the fashions of the day.

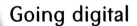

Going digital

Video games emerged in the 1970s, and by 1989 the first Nintendo Game Boy hand-held game consoles were on sale. Better models – with bigger screens and more impressive games – soon appeared, bringing gaming to millions of children who had no access to a desktop computer.

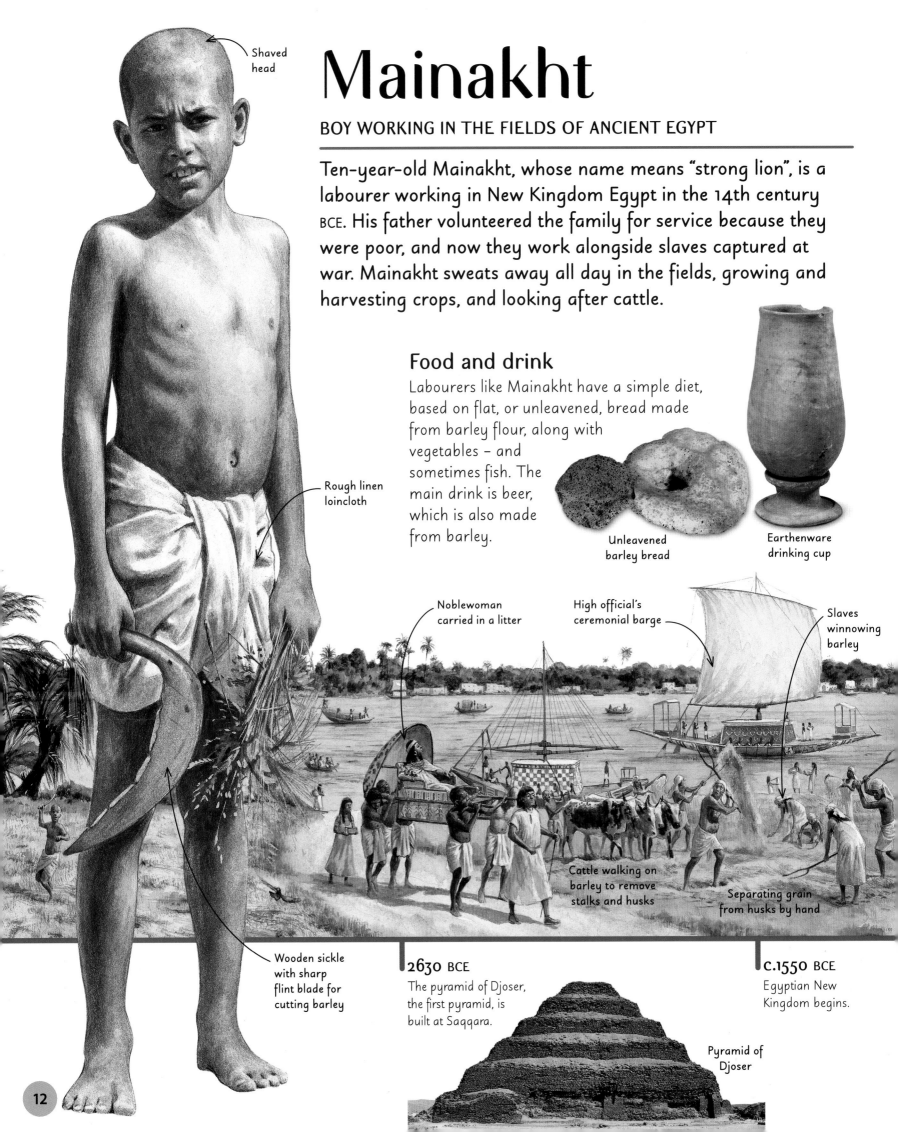

Shaved head

Mainakht

BOY WORKING IN THE FIELDS OF ANCIENT EGYPT

Ten-year-old Mainakht, whose name means "strong lion", is a labourer working in New Kingdom Egypt in the 14th century BCE. His father volunteered the family for service because they were poor, and now they work alongside slaves captured at war. Mainakht sweats away all day in the fields, growing and harvesting crops, and looking after cattle.

Food and drink

Labourers like Mainakht have a simple diet, based on flat, or unleavened, bread made from barley flour, along with vegetables – and sometimes fish. The main drink is beer, which is also made from barley.

Unleavened barley bread

Earthenware drinking cup

Rough linen loincloth

Noblewoman carried in a litter

High official's ceremonial barge

Slaves winnowing barley

Cattle walking on barley to remove stalks and husks

Separating grain from husks by hand

Wooden sickle with sharp flint blade for cutting barley

2630 BCE
The pyramid of Djoser, the first pyramid, is built at Saqqara.

C.1550 BCE
Egyptian New Kingdom begins.

Pyramid of Djoser

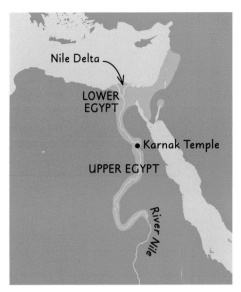

Ancient Egypt

The Egyptians live along the banks of the River Nile. The river floods every year, leaving rich mud on the banks and making the soil fertile. In the dry season, farmers use river water on their crops in the fields.

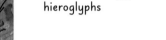

Winnowing

After Mainakht cuts the barley, he separates the grain from the unusable husks, or chaff. To do this he scoops up the grain in pairs of wooden fans, then throws it into the air. The wind blows away the light chaff and the grain falls to the ground.

Wooden fan

Column with Egyptian hieroglyphs

▼ Daily life

Mainakht lives quite close to the river. All the food has to be grown in the fertile flood plain, so the fields are often busy. In the background, boats carry grain, timber, stone, and people between the Nile Delta and Upper Egypt.

Temple of Karnak

Karnak Temple by the Nile is being rebuilt and extended. Boats bring stone along the Nile, and workers build the enormous columns and ceremonial entrances, which are called pylons.

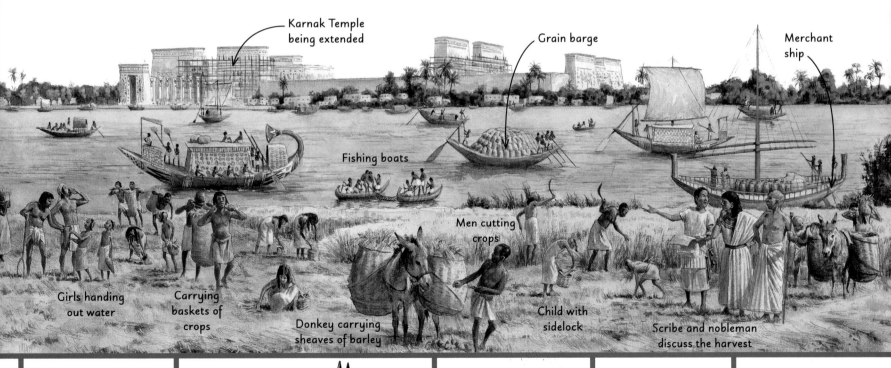

Karnak Temple being extended

Grain barge

Merchant ship

Fishing boats

Men cutting crops

Girls handing out water

Carrying baskets of crops

Donkey carrying sheaves of barley

Child with sidelock

Scribe and nobleman discuss the harvest

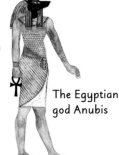

The Egyptian god Anubis

C.1386–1349 BCE
Reign of Pharaoh Amenhotep III. Egypt is at its most powerful.

C.1351–1334 BCE
Pharaoh Akhenaten banishes all the Egyptian gods, except Aten.

C.1279–1213 BCE
Egypt grows powerful in the reign of Ramses II.

C.1155 BCE
Rameses III survives a murder plot made by his wives.

C.1075 BCE
The New Kingdom collapses. Egypt is ruled by different groups of people.

⭐ Real life Tutankhamun

YOUNG KING OF ANCIENT EGYPT

Tutankhamun became king of Egypt in the 14th century BCE, when he was just nine years old. He died aged around 20, and archaeologists discovered his tomb in 1922. Inside, they found his perfectly preserved mummy, surrounded by treasures including furniture and games, which Egyptians believed would be taken into the afterlife.

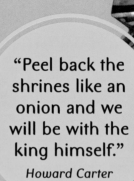

"Peel back the shrines like an onion and we will be with the king himself."
Howard Carter

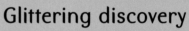

Royal game

This expensive board decorated with gold is from a game called *senet*. The king must have been a keen player, as there were four complete boards in his tomb, as well as the fragments of others.

Glittering discovery

When archaeologists led by Howard Carter opened Tutankhamun's tomb, they were amazed at the riches inside. This glass and gold mask had been placed over the king's head.

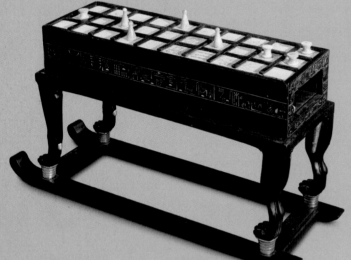

Double kingdom

Tutankhamun ruled over ancient Egypt, which was divided into the two lands of Upper and Lower Egypt along the River Nile. He lived in the city of Waset, which was later renamed Thebes.

LOWER EGYPT

• Waset
UPPER EGYPT

River Nile

Amun →

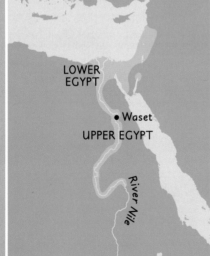

The gods

Tutankhamun's father had stopped people from worshipping most of the old Egyptian gods. The young king reopened their temples and created lots of new art, especially for the king of the gods, Amun.

C.1549–1069 BCE
Period of ancient Egypt known as the New Kingdom.

C.1351 BCE
Tutankhamun's father, Akhenaten, becomes ruler of Egypt.

Akhenaten

C.1340 BCE
Tutankhamun is born. His original name is Tutankhaten.

C.1334 BCE
Akhenaten dies.

C.1332 BCE
Tutankhaten becomes king of Egypt.

Trusty advisers?

Tutankhamun (above) ruled Egypt with the help of advisers. Many of them, like Ay (right), fought each other for the throne when he died.

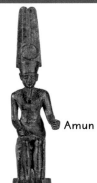

c.1329 BCE
He names himself Tutankhamun after the god Amun.

Amun

c.1329 BCE
Tutankhamun orders building work within Amun's temple at Karnak.

c.1323 BCE
Tutankhamun dies and is buried in the Valley of the Kings.

c.1100–1069 BCE
Graverobbers destroy many tombs, but not Tutankhamun's.

1922 CE
The king's tomb is opened and its contents are revealed.

Classical age

CHAPTER TWO

Great civilizations sprung up around the world from about 800 BCE to 500 CE, including those of the ancient Greeks, ancient Romans, and the Maya in Central America. People built vast cities with temples reaching towards the sky. Complex written languages were developed, but usually only children from rich families went to school.

Amilanu

BOY GROWING UP IN THE ANCIENT CITY OF BABYLON

Ten-year-old Amilanu lives in the city of Babylon in Mesopotamia (now part of Iraq) in 550 BCE. He lives with his parents in a mud-brick house not far from the Euphrates River. His father is a scribe who works for King Nebuchadnezzar II. Because this is an important job, Amilanu's parents can afford for him to go to school to learn mathematics, music, reading, and writing. He is doing well at school and hopes that he will become a scribe like his father.

The Babylonians write on small tablets made of clay. The writing sets when the tablets are dried in the sun.

Ancient maths

Babylonian maths is quite advanced. Amilanu is learning to work in fractions, solve problems, and work out areas and volumes using the rules of geometry.

Ancient Babylonian shapes and numbers

▶ Cuneiform

Amilanu writes using a tool called a stylus made of reed. Pressing it into damp clay makes the wedge-shaped letters that form Babylonian writing. Modern archaeologists call this writing "cuneiform", from a Latin word meaning "wedge-shaped".

Between the rivers

Babylon is one of many large cities in an area called Mesopotamia, which means "the land between the two rivers". The soil here is good for growing crops, and the rivers, the Tigris and the Euphrates, are useful for transport and trade.

• Nineveh

Babylon •

Key

Neo-Babylonian Empire

1894 BCE
The tiny town of Babylon becomes an independent kingdom.

1792–1750 BCE
King Hammurabi creates the first Babylonian Empire.

1595 BCE
The Hittites, from Asia Minor (now Turkey), raid Babylon.

Babylonian gods

The Babylonians worship many different gods and goddesses. One of the most popular is Ishtar. She is empress of the gods and goddess of fertility, love, power, and warfare. Babylon also has a large temple dedicated to Marduk, the main god of the city, which was built in the 18th century BCE.

Clay figure of Ishtar holding a staff and standing on a lion

City of Babylon

Amilanu lives in a city built of bricks. It has moats and a double set of walls around it. It has eight big gates, including the famous Ishtar Gate, which is covered in shiny blue bricks. Beyond are temples, a huge royal palace, and many streets of smaller houses.

IS IT TRUE?

Ancient writers described beautiful "hanging gardens", which were said to have been built in Babylon by King Nebuchadnezzar II. However, modern writers studying other cities believe the idea came from a story about a hillside garden in the city of Nineveh in Mesopotamia. There is no actual evidence for hanging gardens in Babylon.

The gardens were previously thought to be arranged in several layers, like a green mountain.

The tower of Marduk's temple, called a ziggurat

The Ishtar Gate is decorated with lions, symbols of the goddess.

911–627 BCE
The Assyrians, from Assur on the River Tigris, control Babylon.

Assyrian soldiers

626–539 BCE
The Neo-Babylonian period: the city has local rulers.

605–562 BCE
Nebuchadnezzar II is king.

539 BCE
A Persian (modern-day southwest Iran) invasion brings the Babylonian era to an end.

Leonidas

SPARTAN WARRIOR IN TRAINING

Ten-year-old Leonidas lives in Sparta, a city in southeastern Greece, in the 6th century BCE. Like almost all Spartan boys, he left home when he was seven to live at a training camp and learn to become a soldier. His training involves athletics, sports, and weapons practice. He will eventually become a member of one of Europe's most powerful fighting forces.

Women and girls

Unlike other Greek women, Spartan women are educated and allowed to travel around freely. They are encouraged to stay active and healthy so that they give birth to strong children.

Short skirt that is easy to exercise in

Ancient Greece

Sparta rules much of southern Greece. When the army of the Persian Empire invades Greece in 479 BCE, Sparta joins forces with other major city-states, such as Athens, to win the battle.

▼ Training camp

At the camp, Leonidas and the other boys train hard. They sometimes have to live rough to prepare for life in wartime. This can mean sleeping outside, making their own beds from reeds, hunting, or even stealing food.

Warden giving a lesson

Group leader disciplining younger ones with a whip

Javelin practice

Barracks

Marching in formation

Ball game

The boys learn to write using clay tablets.

Group practising spear-handling with wooden poles

c.900 BCE
The settlement of Sparta is built.

7th century BCE
Sparta defeats the neighbouring Messenians, enslaving their people.

Spartan shield with scorpion image

499–449 BCE
The Greeks and the Persians are at war.

464 BCE
Sparta is badly damaged in an earthquake, and the slaves rebel.

Iron-bladed
sword

Spartan boys are
only allowed one
tattered tunic.

Hero worship

As well as worshipping
the traditional Greek gods,
Spartans worship mythical
Greek heroes and heroines.
Menelaus, beloved Spartan
hero and king, has his own
temple called the Menelaion.

Competition and sport

Spartans love sport, especially running,
throwing the discus and javelin, tug
of war, and wrestling. Boys like
Leonidas are encouraged to
play many sports, as this
makes them competitive
and keeps them fit.

Shield bearing image
of Pegasus, a mythical
winged horse

Ancient
Greek discus

Distant temple

Boys sharing
stolen or
foraged food

Adult foot soldier,
or "hoplite"

Collecting
firewood

Boys at the
barracks go
barefoot, even
in winter.

404 BCE
Sparta defeats Athens in
the Peloponnesian Wars.

Early 4th century BCE
Sparta is the most powerful
city in Greece.

362 BCE
After a series of battles
with Thebes, Sparta
begins to lose power.

21

Aurelia

CHILD IN ANCIENT ROME

Aurelia is a ten-year-old girl who lives in the city of Rome at the height of the Roman Empire, in 200 CE. Her father works in a city shop selling cloth and cushions, and the family live in cramped rooms nearby. They are a poor family so, unlike rich Romans, they have no slaves. Aurelia spends most of her time helping her mother to clean their flat, fetching water, doing errands, and looking after her two younger brothers.

Toys

One of Aurelia's favourite toys is a small wooden doll, a simpler version of the ivory doll shown here. Like most Roman children, she also enjoys playing marbles. Her little brother has a model horse on wheels and some toy soldiers.

Model horse

Doll

Roman Empire

The vast Roman Empire is centred around the city of Rome, in present-day Italy, and the Mediterranean Sea. It stretches over much of Europe, as well as parts of north Africa and west Asia.

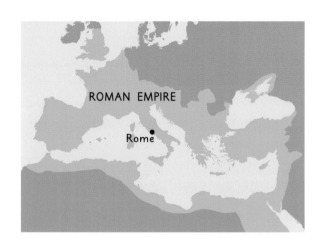

ROMAN EMPIRE

Rome

▼ Going to buy bread

Aurelia lives on a busy street, with lots of shops and bars. When she goes to the bakery, she usually meets children playing in the street, because most people don't have gardens.

A street seller with food

A Roman has his hair cut

Pulling out a tooth

Tutor teaching boys

Cart pulled by oxen

Food bar

Young family slave

Shop selling vegetables

27 BCE
Augustus becomes the first Roman emperor. The empire grows.

Emperor Augustus

64 CE
Much of Rome is destroyed in a fire and the city takes years to rebuild.

106
Emperor Trajan conquers Dacia (modern Romania).

260–270
The Roman Empire shrinks, losing Egypt, Syria, Palestine, and much of Turkey.

Fast food

Like many Romans, Aurelia and her family have no kitchen. She often goes to one of the bars in her area to buy "fast food" such as sausages, fried fish, or meat rissoles, which are a bit like modern burgers.

A Roman food bar

Pendant, called a lunula

Loaf of bread

Boys wear a pendant called a bulla.

Coming of age

Roman girls wear a round or moon-shaped pendant, called a lunula, around the neck. Aurelia will only stop wearing her lunula once she gets married. This is when she will wear adult clothes for the first time.

Hanging out washing

Busy bakery

Shop selling cloth

A rich couple

Beggar

Children playing

Plain white tunic

Leather sandals

293
The empire is divided in two as it is too large for one emperor to rule.

410
Rome is attacked by the Visigoths and the empire loses power.

Replica of ancient Roman plate armour

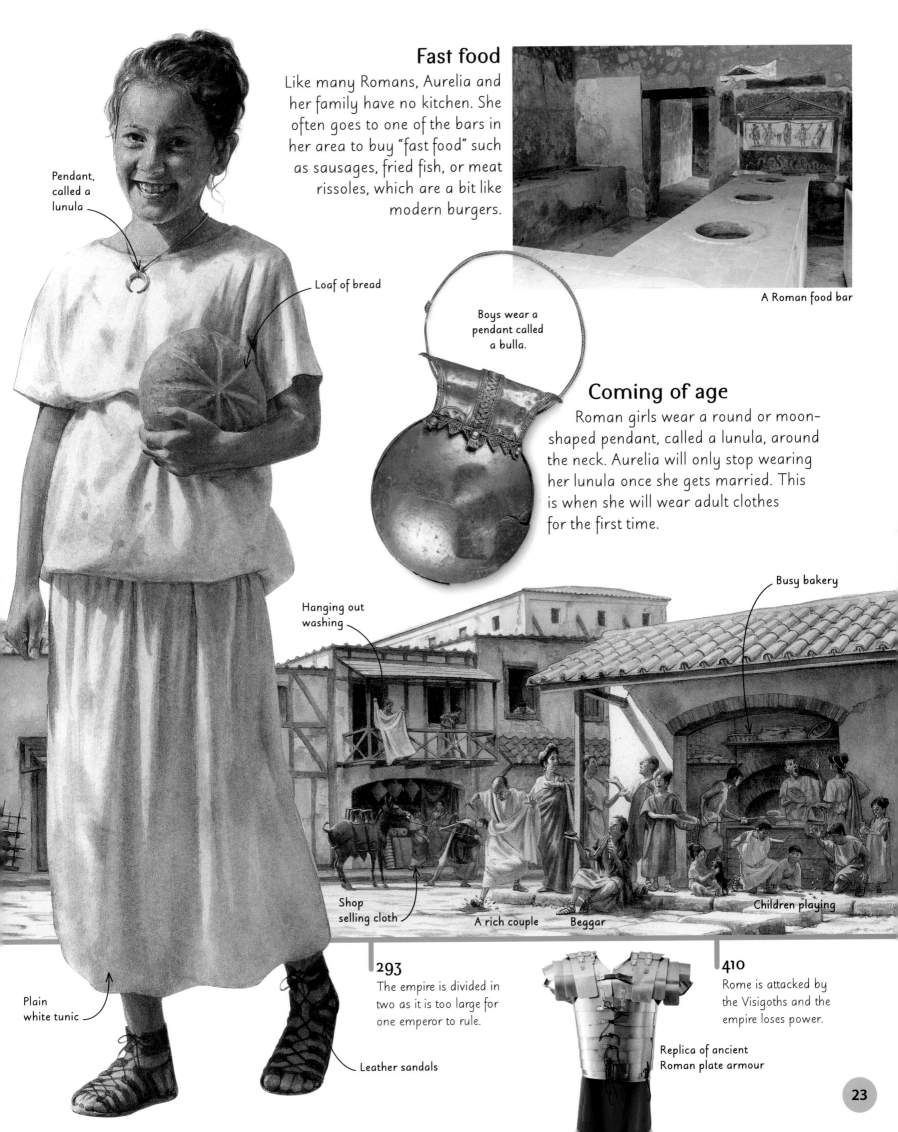

Clothes through time

A JOURNEY THROUGH THE HISTORY OF WHAT PEOPLE WEAR

In ancient times working people dressed simply, while the rich wore expensive clothes made of fine materials. Children often wore the same styles as their parents. Everything changed in the 20th century, when rich people started wearing casual clothes, such as jeans, and owning expensive designer labels became a new kind of status symbol.

Ancient Egypt

Egyptians wore light clothing, often made of linen, to keep cool under the hot African sun. Men wore wraparound skirts with a belt, while women wore long dresses. Children often went naked until about the age of six, then wore similar clothes to their parents.

Wealthy people often wore clothes that were folded into pleats.

Fur trim

Hose

Ancient Greece

A tunic called a "chiton", a square of cloth held together by pins, was the usual choice of clothing in ancient Greece. Women's chitons were ankle-length, while those worn by men and children were shorter. Greeks wore linen in summer and wool in winter, when many people added a cloak.

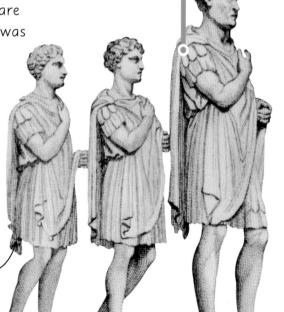

Chiton

Medieval Europe

Clothing varied hugely in the medieval period (400–1400). Women and girls typically wore long dresses. Men wore close-fitting stockings, called "hose", and a loose shirt above the waist. This was sometimes covered by a doublet, which was a buttoned jacket, and a looser coat for warmth. Rich people wore clothes made of finer materials, often with expensive fur.

Cheaper dyes meant more people could wear bright colours in the 19th century.

The Sixties

Modern dress developed in the 20th century, with different types of clothing for work and comfortable casual wear. Different styles of clothes for children also appeared. The 1960s was a period of brightly coloured fabrics, when items such as jeans and T-shirts became popular and skirts for women and girls became much shorter.

Colourful, patterned T-shirts were popular in the 1960s.

19th century

This century saw elaborate long dresses for women and girls become popular. Often they were narrow at the waist, with full skirts held up by a frame of hoops beneath, or with lots of petticoats. Men and boys started wearing trousers.

The Renaissance

Long dresses, often with detachable sleeves, were popular for women and girls in the Renaissance period (1400–1550). Men and boys continued to wear doublets and hose. Rich people wore luxury fabrics, such as velvets.

Modern day

In the last few decades fashions have changed quickly, with clothes transported all over the world. There are fewer rules about what to wear, and more people are able to choose what they like.

Each year, more than 80 billion items of clothing are made worldwide.

Ellac

YOUNG HUN AT THE TIME OF ATTILA

Ellac is a 12-year-old boy who lives with his extended family in eastern Europe in around 450 CE. His people are Huns, who migrated here a few decades ago and have united under their powerful leader, Attila. The Huns are often on the move to graze their livestock on new grassland or raid enemy territory. A Hun boy like Ellac has to be tough and able to ride a horse. He is already a good shot with a bow and arrow.

Hun cauldrons usually have mushroom-shaped handles.

Bronze cauldron

Ellac's family eat boiled meat for their main meal. They cook it over a fire in a cauldron made of cast bronze. The Huns are skilled metalworkers, and it is easy to recognize their cauldrons, which have a tall, round base.

Tall base so cauldron can stand in the middle of a fire

Attila the Hun

Attila, the most successful Hun leader of all time, rules in the mid-5th century. He leads his people in huge armed raids, attacking nearby cities and even reaching as far as Germany and Gaul (France). His aim is to capture booty, not to take over lands.

This engraving shows Attila in ceremonial clothes, though ancient writers say he dressed simply.

Famous long beard

HUNNIC EMPIRE

BLACK SEA

Lands and journeys

The Huns are originally from the steppes, an area of grassland northeast of the Black Sea. By Attila's time, they are based in eastern Europe, from where they send raiding armies towards Greece, France, and Germany. Their always-shifting empire does not have fixed borders.

376 CE
Huns invade the Ukrainian steppes from the east.

395
Huns launch first attack on the Eastern Roman Empire.

Attila leads the Huns into battle

437
Brothers Attila and Bleda become the Huns' joint rulers.

Animals in art

The Huns see many different kinds of animals on their travels, and their artists show these creatures in their art. Horses and deer are favourite subjects. Metalworkers make decorative pieces in bronze, sometimes also coating them with gold.

The top of the bow is longer than the bottom, making it easier to use on horseback.

Some experts think Hun boys had their faces scarred to show grief after the death of a family member.

Leather hat trimmed with fur for warmth

Arrow with bone tip sharpened to a point

Precious metals

The Huns like gold jewellery. They either wear it or use it to decorate their horses' harnesses. Some is made from plundered Roman gold, while some is taken from jewellery of the Germanic tribes that the Huns target on their raids.

Gold headband inlaid with coloured glass and gemstones

Arrows in quiver

The Huns rode without stirrups.

▶ A boy and his horse

Ellac learned to ride and to look after his horse when he was a small boy. Horses are vital to the Huns: they are used to ride into battle and also as a source of milk. Ellac is very proud of his bow – he made it himself.

Calf-length leather boots

445–453
Attila is sole ruler of the Huns after the death of his brother (whom he may have murdered).

449
The Romans agree to give the Huns regular tribute, or pay, in gold.

454
The Gepids, an east Germanic tribe, defeat the Huns in battle, ending their dominance.

Medieval period

CHAPTER THREE

Powerful empires ruled large parts of the globe from the 5th to the 15th centuries CE. Most children worked with their parents or stayed at home doing chores. Religion was an important part of people's lives, and huge cathedrals and mosques were built.

Ixchel

MAYA GIRL LIVING IN A FARMING COMMUNITY

Ten-year-old Ixchel lives in southeastern Mexico at the beginning of the 7th century CE, when the Maya rule the region. Like most Maya women and girls, she has not been to school. Her father is a farmer, but Ixchel and her mother are skilled weavers, and spend most of their time at their looms, creating beautiful, brightly coloured cloth.

Hair tied into plaits

Pattern woven into the fabric

Brightly coloured yarn for weaving

Dress called a *huipil*, made of cotton and hemp

Tool, called a shuttle, used for weaving

Maya world

Maya land stretches from southeastern Mexico, across Guatemala and Belize, and into parts of El Salvador and Honduras. Much of the area is mountainous, with flatter land nearer the coast.

Palenque • • Chichén Itzá
• Tikal
• Copán

Maya civilization, 7th century CE

Terraced fields, cut into hillside

Decorated temple

House with thatched roof and mud walls

Planting maize

Storing corn

Preparing food

300 BCE
Maya civilization starts to flourish. Many Maya cities are built.

426 CE
K'inich Yax K'uk' Mo becomes ruler of the city of Copán, Honduras.

500
Tikal becomes the largest Maya city. It is home to around 50,000 people.

Young maize god

Maize, or corn, is an important food crop for the Maya. Ixchel worships the maize god Hun Hunahpu, and believes the first people were made of maize.

Headdress of corn cobs

Maya calendar

Maya mathematicians and astronomers devised a calendar based on two cycles of dates and 13 numbered days. Together, these create a calendar that starts again at the beginning every 52 years.

Pictures, or hieroglyphs, represent the months.

Hieroglyphs representing the days

▼ Temples

Temples, where the gods are worshipped, are often the tallest buildings in towns and cities. Ixchel's family believe that the gods influence almost everything in their daily lives.

Hieroglyphs

The Maya use a system of writing based on pictorial symbols, called hieroglyphs. The hieroglyphs on this stone carving identify the Maya king, Shield Jaguar II (681–742 CE), and his wife, Lady Xoc.

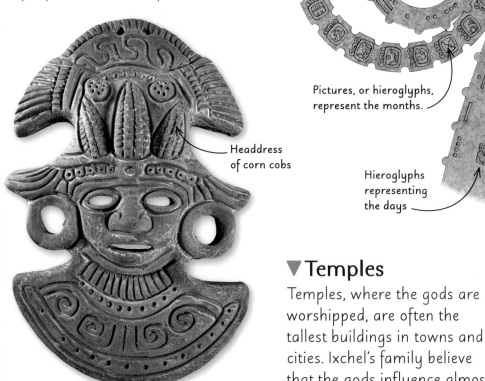

Main temple set high up on a stepped limestone platform

Boys playing a Maya ball game

Dense tropical jungle

Coating walls with mud

Warrior

Group of prisoners arriving in the village

Wealthy couple

Women weaving cloth

615
Pakal the Great is made ruler of the great Maya city-state of Palenque.

9th century
Drought leads to the abandonment of many Maya cities.

1000
Chichén Itzá on Mexico's Yucatán Peninsula becomes an important Maya cultural centre.

Remains of Chichén Itzá

1524
The Spanish conquer the Maya region.

Snofrida

CHILD IN A VIKING VILLAGE

Snofrida is a ten-year-old girl living in tenth-century Norway. Her father is a farmer, but he also serves the local lord. The lord settles arguments between people and protects Snofrida's family from raiders. Last summer Snofrida's elder brother went with the lord across the sea to fight in England. He came back with a lot of money – and a few cuts and bruises. Most of Snofrida's time is spent cooking with her mother, or spinning wool into thread using a spindle and distaff.

Distaff with wool

Braided hair

Family necklace

Spindle

Home by the water

Snofrida's family live in Hladir. This is a village on the shore of Trondheim Fjord, where the sea meets the mountains. In the winter it is dark for 20 hours every day and the temperature stays below freezing for weeks on end. But the summers are lovely and warm.

Hladir

Farmer leading ox

Loading a boat with goods

Net drying

Turfed roof

Women discussing the village feast

A bard telling stories to children

c.750 CE
The Vikings increase their territory in Scandinavia.

793
Viking warriors visit England for the first time.

c.870
Vikings begin to settle in Iceland.

Viking sword and shield

Mealtime

Stew is Snofrida's favourite meal. It is made by boiling cheese, vegetables, and butter with oatmeal. Sometimes they add fish from the fjord. On special days they have roasted pork or lamb. In the autumn Snofrida picks large amounts of fruit, such as apples, plums, and blackberries.

Cabbage

Water

Butter

Leek

Cheese

Oatmeal

Viking ships

When travelling to nearby villages, Snofrida's family go by sea to avoid the steep mountains and dense forests. Merchants use larger ships to travel longer distances, while warriors use fast ships, such as this one, so they can take people by surprise.

Ships are sometimes adorned with dragon heads.

Shields protect warriors inside the ship.

▼ Fjord life

The soil in Hladir is thin and produces poor crops. The Vikings spend much of their time herding sheep or fishing. In the winter they weave cloth or trap animals for their fur. The cloth and fur is sold to traders who sail here in the spring.

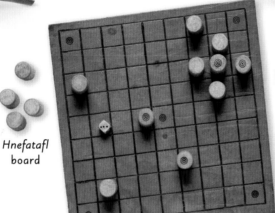

Hnefatafl board

Family games

Snofrida's father and brother enjoy playing *hnefatafl*, a board game that uses a square board and pieces to represent warriors. Snofrida prefers to play a dice game called Fox and Geese.

Fish from the fjord hanging out to dry

Boys practising sword skills

The lord's hall, the centre of the village

Lord discussing the approaching ships

Shepherd herding sheep

Longship being rowed out to sea

Longhouse

Girls carrying water

Warriors

911
Rollo conquers Normandy in France.

c.980
The first Viking settlement in Greenland is established.

c.1000
Leif Erikson becomes the first European to set foot in North America.

Leif Erikson

1013
Sweyn Forkbeard becomes king of England after a 12-year war.

1066
Death of Harald Hardrada in England ends the age of Viking conquests.

Bernhard

KNIGHT'S SQUIRE IN MEDIEVAL EUROPE

Bernhard is a 12-year-old boy from near Bamberg, where he was born in 1055. Like other boys with rich parents, he was sent at the age of seven to another family's castle to work as a page, assisting a knight with simple tasks. Five years later he became a squire, or knight's assistant, training for battle and tending to the knight's horses and armour. Bernhard practises with a sword and bow, likes to ride, and wants to be a knight one day.

Medieval Germany

In the Middle Ages, Germany is not a single country, but is made up of many small states and cities. Each is ruled by its own lord, but under the overall rule of the Holy Roman Emperor. Bamberg, in Bavaria, southern Germany, is one of these states.

Heavy blade

Weaponry

A knight's main weapon is his sword. It is a handmade weapon with a double-edged blade. It also has a cross guard to protect the user's hand from his opponent's sword. The knight uses it with a slashing motion, both on horseback and on foot.

The wooden tower is a refuge in times of war.

Tower guard

A hunting party gets ready to leave the castle

Falcon

Workshop of fletcher (arrow-maker)

Blacksmith's workshop

The tower is built on a mound.

Sword practice

9th century
Armoured men on horseback often take part in warfare.

11th century
Knights, who swear allegiance to a lord or king, become common in Europe.

c.1050–1500
Knights are at their most powerful.

Armoured knight and horse

c.1300
Some knights wear armour made of metal plates.

c.1350
Primitive canons are used in warfare in Europe.

Armour

Mail is made of interlinked rings of metal.

In the 11th century, a knight's main protection is a coat of mail. If Bernhard rides into battle with his knight, he will also wear mail. It prevents sword cuts, but it is very heavy to wear.

Undyed undertunic

Woollen tunic

Arrows with wooden shafts, sharp metal tips, and feather fletching

Leather grip

Horses

Bernhard's knight has four horses – two warhorses, which are well built and can gallop for long stretches; a swift mount for hunting; and an older one for travelling. Bernhard keeps their harnesses and shoes in good order.

Horseshoe

▼ Castle

The castle is mostly built of wood. It is both home and workplace for the knight and his family, servants, and craftsmen. They live and work in the buildings in the bailey, or castle yard.

Castle chapel

Thatcher fixes a roof

Tall wooden palisades (fences) protect the castle from attackers.

Milk maid

Man in stocks

Leather shoes

c.1400
Suits of metal-plate armour become fashionable.

Armoured glove, or gauntlet

c.1600
Professional soldiers are used more widely, so knights lose their fighting role.

The Crusades

MEDIEVAL WARS IN THE HOLY LAND

The Crusades were religious wars in the eastern Mediterranean area during medieval times. This area was known in Europe as the Holy Land, and was sacred to Christians, Muslims, and Jews. Armies of Christians from Europe, called crusaders, fought to take control of the Holy Land from the Muslims living there. Most of these attempts failed, including a Crusade by children.

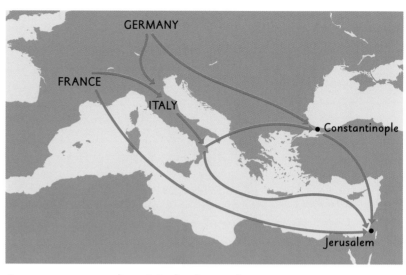

Journey to the Holy Land

The crusaders came from various European countries, including England, France, and Germany. Their journey to the Holy Land took them through Europe and across the Mediterranean Sea. Constantinople, now Istanbul in Turkey, was ruled by Christian emperors of the Byzantine Empire, who supported some of the crusades, but not all.

The First Crusade (1096–1099)

Pope Urban II, leader of the Roman Catholic Church, launched the First Crusade. The crusaders captured Jerusalem, the main city in the Holy Land, and set up small states, such as Edessa and Antioch, to keep control of the region.

Soldiers of the First Crusade

Crusader knights

The Second Crusade (1147–1149)

After Muslim forces captured the crusaders' state of Edessa, the Second Crusade was launched in Europe. Many people joined the army, but the Crusade was poorly organized and didn't have much money, so the army failed to take back the land.

638
Christian Byzantine Empire loses Jerusalem to Muslim forces.

1095
Pope Urban II launches the First Crusade at Clermont, France.

Crusader's helmet

1098
Edessa and Antioch (in modern-day Turkey and Syria) become the first crusader states.

1144
Edessa is captured by Muslim forces, sparking the Second Crusade.

Children's Crusade

In 1212, thousands of European children marched on a Crusade towards Jerusalem. The French children were led by Stephen of Cloyes, a 12-year-old shepherd boy. This Crusade ended in tragedy, as most children died of hunger, and some were captured and became slaves.

Saladin

The Sultan of Egypt, Saladin, was a Muslim military leader. He gathered support from the nearby countries of Syria and Egypt, and they attacked Christians occupying the Holy Land. They reconquered Jerusalem in 1187.

Saladin

Stephen of Cloyes

Destruction of Constantinople

In the early 1200s, there was a struggle for power in southern Europe. In 1204, the army of the Fourth Crusade conquered and destroyed parts of the beautiful city of Constantinople, stealing from the houses and churches.

Kerak Castle, captured by Saladin in 1189

1189–1192
The Third Crusade fails to defeat the Muslims.

1202–1204
The Fourth Crusade never reaches Jerusalem.

1217–1221
The Fifth Crusade tries to conquer the Muslim state of Egypt, but fails.

1291
The last crusader city, Acre, falls to the Muslims. Most Europeans leave the Holy Land.

Takeshi

TRAINEE SAMURAI WARRIOR IN 12TH-CENTURY JAPAN

Takeshi is a Japanese boy from an upper-class family who is training to become a samurai warrior. He starts his preparation in the year 1109, when he is 13 years old. He has to learn a range of skills – such as swordsmanship, horse riding, and the martial art of *jujitsu*. He spends most of his time in this training, and also learns about the religion of Buddhism and the importance it places on honour and loyalty. These are the values of the samurai.

Tachi, a type of long samurai sword used in the 11th century

Samurai beliefs

All samurai believe they should always be loyal to their lord, and many are Buddhists. Buddhists practise meditation, and Takeshi's family make regular trips to the local Buddhist temple.

A jacket with wide sleeves allows a good range of movement while sword fighting.

Sash holding sheath in place

Buddhist temple built in the 10th century

Trousers called *hakama* are tied at the waist and go down to the ankle.

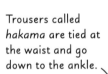

Rice-straw sandals

794
Start of the Heian period, during which Buddhism grows popular in Japan.

Buddha statue, Tokyo, Japan

c.806
Forces led by local samurai lords grow more powerful after Emperor Kammu disbands his army.

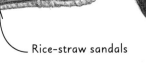

Samurai swords

When he is fully armed, Takeshi has two swords, one long and one short. Both are made by hand by master craftsmen, and are as sharp as razors. Takeshi has to train hard to make sure he uses them properly and safely.

Short samurai sword called a *wakazashi*

◄ Learning to fight

Takeshi goes to a special school where boys learn the way of the samurai warrior. As well as skills like swordsmanship and shooting a moving target with a bow, Takeshi studies subjects such as history and literature.

Wooden sheath for sword

Armour

Takeshi's father gave him his first suit of armour when he was five years old. The armour is made of overlapping metal plates and held together securely with laces.

High-ranking men like this military leader had fancy and colourful armour.

Calligraphy commissioned by the Japanese emperor

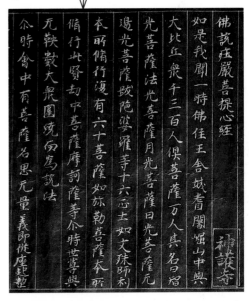

JAPAN

Japanese clans

Japan is a collection of islands, with clans, or groups, holding power in their areas. Samurai protect the local clan rulers from rivals and grow powerful in the emperor of Japan's court.

Calligraphy

Takeshi has to learn to read and write. He is expected to practise the art of calligraphy – beautiful writing – using a brush and ink. Skill in calligraphy is valued very highly in Japan.

10th century	**1192**	**1281**	**14th century**	**1543**
Samurai warrior families such as the Fujiwara, Taira, and Minamoto become powerful.	Minamoto no Yoritomo becomes shogun (military leader), ruling for the emperor.	Samurai, helped by a typhoon (strong winds), defend Japan against Mongol invaders.	A metalworker called Masamune improves the sharpness and strength of samurai swords.	Larger armies and the use of firearms mean the end of Samurai warfare.

The Mongols

A HUGE EMPIRE LED BY A FAMOUS RULER

In the 13th century, Genghis Khan united the people living on the grasslands of central Asia and formed a huge army. They fought their way across Asia and into Europe and created one of history's biggest empires. Horses helped them move with great speed, and virtually all Mongolian children learned to ride.

A supportive saddle helps the horseman to ride hands-free so that he can draw his bow.

Horseback warriors

Children learned to ride from the age of three, and boys practised archery as soon as they could draw a bow. Armed with deadly skills, boys often grew up to be fearsome warriors.

Genghis Khan

Genghis Khan (c.1162–1227) conquered a huge amount of land, often winning battles where his armies were outnumbered. He did not rule the whole empire himself but created vassal states – countries that had to pay him taxes.

Mongol Empire

The Mongol Empire stretched from central Europe to the Far East. The Mongols founded China's Yuan dynasty, which ruled for almost a century, from 1271 to 1368.

RUSSIA
EUROPE **ASIA**
CHINA

c.1130
Chinese Jin dynasty repel attacks by the Mongols.

c.1200
Mongolian climate warms, bringing lusher grass for livestock to feed on.

Livestock

1206
Genghis Khan becomes ruler of the Mongols.

1227
Genghis Khan dies.

1259
Quarrels in the royal family lead to the breakup of the empire into different sections, or "khanates".

Protective helmet

Protecting merchants

Trade routes linking China with Europe crossed the empire. Mongols protected merchants but charged taxes for passing through. These routes were called the "Silk Road". Valuable Chinese silk was among the goods traded.

Mongolian metal armour

Looking after animals

Mongol families kept animals such as sheep and goats for meat, milk, and wool. They herded the animals from one place to another to keep them fattened up on different pastures. Children helped out with both herding and milking the animals.

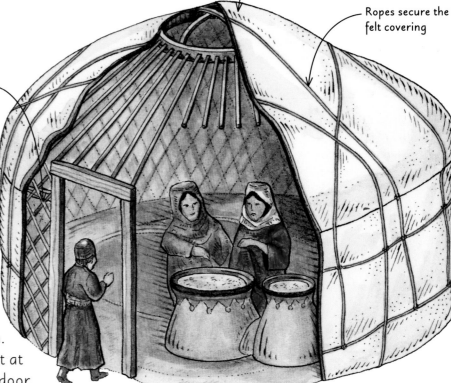

Thick covering of woollen felt

Ropes secure the felt covering

Frame made of bent wooden strips and poles

Mongolian tents

Mongolian families moved around a lot. They lived in round tents called *gers*, which were quick to put up and take down. The tent was divided so that the seniors sat at the back, while the juniors sat nearest the door.

1260
Mongols beaten by Muslim Mamluk forces at the Battle of Ain Jalut, Galilee.

1260
Kublai Khan names himself Great Khan, leader of the Mongols.

1271
Kublai founds the Yuan dynasty in China.

1368
Yuan dynasty falls. Mongol power is in decline.

1405
Timur, last major Mongol ruler, dies.

Mongol warrior bow

The Silk Road

TRADE ROUTES FROM EAST TO WEST

The Silk Road was a number of overland routes that linked China with Europe. These routes were used to transport goods for trading, especially between the 2nd century BCE and the 15th century CE. The route also meant exciting new ideas and inventions could be shared. Children living along the Silk Road would have witnessed passing merchants from all over Asia and Europe with a variety of interesting items for sale.

The route

The Silk Road crossed central Asia, through areas with different cultures and languages, including Chinese, Persian, Armenian, Turkish, and Greek. As well as bringing goods to Europe, merchants traded between the countries of Asia.

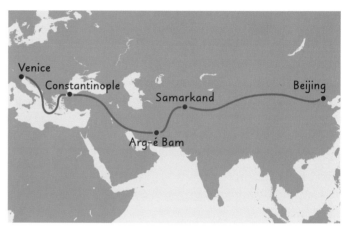

How to make silk was kept secret by the Chinese for many centuries.

Arg-é Bam

The walled city of Arg-é Bam, in what is now southeastern Iran, was at a crossroads where the routes joined. In the city, lots of merchants traded their goods.

Two-way trade

European merchants traded gold and silver for expensive goods from Asia. Persian merchants had dates, nuts, and saffron to sell. Other merchants sold spices that only grew in Asia, such as cinnamon and nutmeg, as well as silks and pottery.

Alexander the Great

C.475 BCE
Persian Royal Road links Persia (Iran) to the east Mediterranean.

329 BCE
Alexander the Great leads Greek exploration of central Asia.

C.138 BCE
Chinese explorer Zhang Qian is sent out by the Chinese emperor to explore Asia.

C.130 BCE
The Silk Road is established after Zhang Qian's expedition.

Life on the road

Merchants used camels to carry goods and supplies of food and water. They used both two-humped Bactrian camels and single-humped dromedaries. They travelled in large groups called caravans for safety, as robbers could attack them along the route.

Mud-brick walls of Arg-é Bam

A new way of trading

In the 15th century, the English and Portuguese in western Europe wanted to be able to trade directly with eastern Asia. Instead of travelling overland, the merchants sailed across the ocean. The Silk Road was no longer so important.

6th century CE
Spies steal silkworm eggs from China. Silk is made in the West and the Silk Road goes into decline.

Silkworm

639 CE
Silk Road in use again under the Chinese Tang Dynasty.

1207–1360
Silk Road trade booms under the Mongol Empire in China.

1490s onwards
Importance of the Silk Road declines as European merchants favour sea routes.

Food through time

A JOURNEY THROUGH THE HISTORY OF EATING

For most of history, people ate what they could gather, hunt, or produce by farming. There were no fridges or freezers until the 19th century, so people mostly ate fresh food. In the 19th and 20th centuries, tinned and frozen food became available, giving people access to a wider range of tasty foods.

Goat's cheese

Ancient Greeks stored olive oil in huge pottery jars.

Olives

Stone Age

Axe

In the early Stone Age people hunted and gathered food such as leaves, berries, and eggs when they could be found. Children were taught what to pick and how to hunt by adults. Farming began in the later Stone Age.

Red mullet

Ancient Greece

The ancient Greeks (5th century BCE onwards) were good at boat-building, so they could fish in the sea and buy food abroad. However, most people ate local produce, such as olives and cheese made from goat's milk, and drank wine made from local grapes.

Nettles

Birds' eggs

Medieval feast

During the medieval period (400–1400), farming provided a diet of bread made from wheat, plus a range of crops. The rich feasted on meats, from venison to wild boar, but poor families mostly ate vegetables.

Age of Exploration

Between the 15th and 17th centuries, European explorers brought spices from Asia, coffee from Turkey, and a huge range of foods – including tomatoes and potatoes – from the Americas. For many, food became much more varied and exciting.

Coffee beans

Food was canned years before anyone invented a can opener!

Packaged foods

Tinned and frozen foods, introduced in the 19th century, became cheap and popular in the 20th century. This meant that people were able to enjoy "seasonal" vegetables all through the year, and could keep food for months without it going off.

Health and variety

Modern scientific research has revealed how important it is to eat a balanced, varied diet, with lots of fresh fruit and vegetables. Avoiding sugary sweets and drinks, and not eating too much fat, helps keep children and adults healthy.

Teresa

GIRL LIVING AT THE TIME OF THE BLACK DEATH

Teresa is a 12-year-old girl who lives in Barcelona, Spain, during the great plague of 1348. Her father is a merchant, and the family's life has been devastated by the plague. Many of their friends have caught the disease. Victims have a fever, dark swellings on their skin, and die within a few days.

The Black Death

People call the plague the "Black Death". There is no cure and people do not realize it is carried on fleas, which live on rats and other animals, and thrive in dirty towns and cities.

Merchant ship

Teresa's father trades goods that come to Barcelona on ships that sail around the Mediterranean Sea. Vessels from Italian cities such as Genoa and Venice bring silk cloth, spices, salt, wheat, leather goods, and furs.

▼ Street in Barcelona

With its many shops and merchants' warehouses, Barcelona was once a busy city. Now there are just sick people, with others carrying the dead to be buried.

Scrubbing a doorstep with vinegar to try to protect the home from the plague

Cart carrying dead bodies

Burning a victim's clothes to try to prevent the illness spreading

Children praying for the plague to end

A priest with a dying man

1320s
Outbreaks of plague are reported in China.

1347
Plague reaches southern Italy, and Marseilles, France.

1348–1349
The disease travels to Barcelona, England, Africa, and Arabia.

1350
One-third to one-half of the population of affected countries has died.

14–17th centuries
Further outbreaks of plague affect Europe.

Spread of the plague

The plague spread over land trade routes from China to the Black Sea. Ships from the Genoese port of Kaffa then carried the disease to the Mediterranean and into Europe. Other land-based traders took it into Africa and the Middle East.

ASIA

EUROPE

Barcelona

BLACK SEA

AFRICA

Key

Areas affected by the plague

Wormwood is used to treat sickness.

Herbal medicine

Doctors use herbs to combat disease, but these don't cure people of the plague, which people think is God's punishment for their sins. Some herbs help to ease a few of the symptoms of the plague.

Underdress, or "kirtle"

Holding wooden rosary beads while praying for the sick

Long overdress, or "cote-hardie"

Feverfew is used to combat fever and headaches.

Monks carry the statue of a saint in a religious procession

Bunches of herbs as protection from infection

Cross marks the house of a sufferer

1720
Europe's last major plague epidemic occurs in Marseilles.

1900–1925
Outbreaks in Australia lead researchers to discover that fleas carry the disease.

Flea

47

Li Sheng

BOY GROWING UP DURING THE MING DYNASTY

Li Sheng is a nine-year-old boy who lives in Nanjing, China, at the beginning of the Ming dynasty (1368–1644). His family is big and he is especially close to his father and elder brother. Li Sheng and his brother both go to school where they study the ideas of the philosopher Confucius and learn how to read and write Chinese. They are doing well in school so will probably get jobs working for the Ming dynasty like their father.

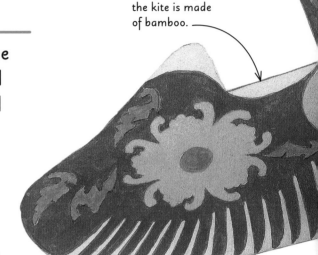

The frame of the kite is made of bamboo.

The kite is covered with brightly painted silk fabric.

Key

 Extent of the Ming dynasty, 1400

China in the Ming period

The Ming emperors protect their empire with a large army and rebuild the Great Wall to defend its borders. To run the empire, they have many people working for the government, in what is called the civil service. Li Sheng hopes that when he is older he will pass the exams to get into the civil service.

Confucianism

Li Sheng's parents bring him up to believe in the values of Confucius. Confucius taught that family values were the most important of all: children should respect their parents, be loyal to them, and care for them when they need it.

Confucian temple, Beijing

1368
The Hongwu Emperor founds the Ming dynasty.

1402–1424
The Yongle Emperor strengthens Ming power and builds Beijing's Forbidden City.

Statue of the Yongle Emperor, Beijing

1405–1433
Chinese sailor Zheng He explores the Indian Ocean and the South China Sea.

1421
Beijing becomes China's capital.

◀ Toys and games

Chinese children like activities such as wrestling and martial arts, skipping, and hide and seek. They also play with kites and puppets. Li Sheng's kite is his favourite toy. Kites were invented in China, and Li Sheng's is shaped like a bird.

Soft fabric cap

Silk robe with wide sleeves

Reel holds the kite string

Loose silk trousers

Noodles

Carp

Fresh food

Li Sheng eats a lot of different foods. As well as common foods like noodles, rice, and sesame cakes, he eats fish, such as carp or bream. He also likes fruit such as plums, apricots, and cherries.

Green plums

Sesame cake

The wall is built of large stone blocks.

Nanjing city wall

Nanjing is the capital of China in the early Ming period and is probably the world's largest city. The first Ming emperor has just rebuilt much of the city, and he has built strong stone walls for protection.

1450
The Great Wall is strengthened after a northeastern attack from a group of Mongols called Oirats.

16th century
China begins to trade with Europe more.

1644
The Ming rulers are replaced by a new dynasty, the Qing.

Tlahco

CHILD LIVING IN THE AZTEC CITY OF TENOCHTITLAN

Tlahco is a ten-year-old girl living in the Aztec city of Tenochtitlan during the 15th century. Her father, a farmer, grows tomatoes, beans, squash, and maize in small fields on the edge of the city. In Aztec society women are active and well respected. Tlahco trades goods at the local market and is learning how to make jewellery. Like all Aztec girls, as soon as she is a teenager Tlahco will go to school to learn about subjects such as history and religion.

Home skills

Tlahco learns the skills she will need as an adult by helping her mother. She is shown how to weave cloth, cook, and grind maize into flour on a grinding stone called a *metlatl*.

The Aztec world

The Aztecs live in the Valley of Mexico, a high-up, flat area in the centre of Mexico. Tenochtitlan is the largest Aztec city, and the capital of the empire.

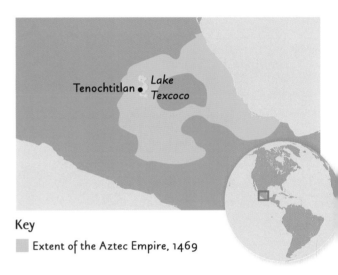

Tenochtitlan • Lake Texcoco

Key

Extent of the Aztec Empire, 1469

▼ Floating city

Tenochtitlan is built on an island in Lake Texcoco. It is criss-crossed with busy canals and surrounded by *chinampas*, small areas of fertile man-made islands where Tlahco's father farms. Each district of Tenochtitlan has its own market.

Porters carry packs of cacao beans

Officials wearing brightly coloured cloth made from plant fibres

Pyramid topped with temples for two gods

Busy market

c.1248
Aztec people settle by Lake Texcoco.

c.1325
City of Tenochtitlan is founded.

1428
Tenochtitlan and two other cities form the basis of the Aztec Empire.

Aztec eagle warrior

1440–1469
Moctezuma I expands the empire and develops Tenochtitlan's laws and culture.

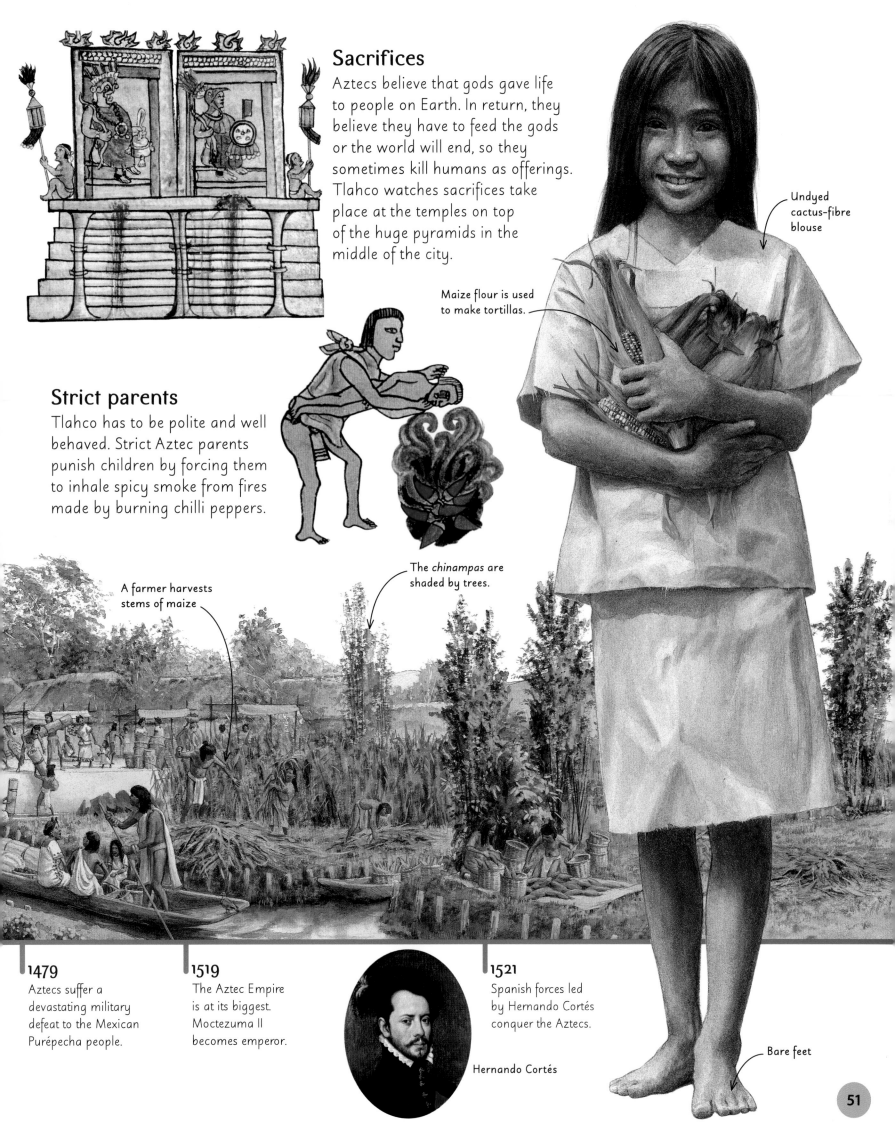

Sacrifices

Aztecs believe that gods gave life to people on Earth. In return, they believe they have to feed the gods or the world will end, so they sometimes kill humans as offerings. Tlahco watches sacrifices take place at the temples on top of the huge pyramids in the middle of the city.

Undyed cactus-fibre blouse

Maize flour is used to make tortillas.

Strict parents

Tlahco has to be polite and well behaved. Strict Aztec parents punish children by forcing them to inhale spicy smoke from fires made by burning chilli peppers.

The *chinampas* are shaded by trees.

A farmer harvests stems of maize

1479
Aztecs suffer a devastating military defeat to the Mexican Purépecha people.

1519
The Aztec Empire is at its biggest. Moctezuma II becomes emperor.

1521
Spanish forces led by Hernando Cortés conquer the Aztecs.

Hernando Cortés

Bare feet

Su-gyeong
CHILD IN KOREA DURING THE JOSEON PERIOD

Su-gyeong, aged 11, lives in Hanseong, the capital city of Joseon (Korea) in the 1470s. There are not many good jobs available to girls, but they can become doctors who treat other women. This is because physical contact is not allowed between unmarried men and women, even during medical treatment. Su-gyeong's father is a doctor, and she is learning how to heal people, too.

Short *jeogori* jacket tied with a ribbon

Pestle and mortar for grinding herbs used as medicines

◄ Doctor in training

Su-gyeong goes to a health clinic to train in traditional medicine. She learns about twin forces inside the body called yin and yang. She is shown how to balance these forces to cure sickness.

Acupuncture needles and burnt mugwort

Traditional medicine

Joseon doctors use special techniques to heal people. During acupuncture, needles are inserted into the patient's body. Burning mugwort herbs are also held over parts of the body in a technique called moxibustion.

Long, full *chima* skirt made of silk

1392
Having defeated various rivals, King Taejo founds the Joseon dynasty.

1418–1450
Technology and science advance during the reign of Seong the Great.

Living in Joseon

The rule of Korea's Joseon kings began in 1392 and lasted more than 500 years. Hanseong, later called Seoul, is the capital city of Joseon. The success of the country depends on trade and relations with their powerful neighbours, China and Japan.

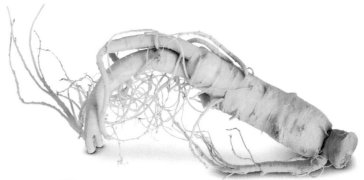

Ginseng

When Su-gyeong is ill, she drinks a mixture containing the root of a plant called ginseng. Joseon doctors believe it gives people strength. Ginseng grows wild in Joseon, and people gather it to trade with their Chinese neighbours.

Sundial invented by the scientist Jang Yeong-sil

Painting on fine Korean silk

Porcelain perfume bottle

Science and technology

Astronomy, the study of stars and planets, flourishes around Su-gyeong's time. People are able to pinpoint the positions of planets in the sky. Joseon scholars invent ways to tell the time, such as special sundials and water clocks, and draw up improved maps.

Joseon goods

People in Joseon Korea become rich through trading products such as silk, porcelain, and jewellery with other countries. They trade lots of items with the Japanese island of Tushima, and Tushima's people help to keep the seas clear of pirates.

Letter seal with Hangul characters

1443
Hangul, the Korean alphabet, is introduced.

1592–1598
Japan launches several invasions of Joseon Korea.

1636
The Manchu invade Korea from China.

c.1650–1850
Korea enjoys a period of peace.

1897
Joseon period ends and the Korean Empire is founded.

Early modern period

CHAPTER FOUR

Huge changes took place between the 16th and 18th centuries. Art and education boomed during the Renaissance, and new Christian Protestant churches were founded as part of the Reformation. Slavery also became a horrible reality for millions of African people, including many children.

Alvaro

CHILD WORKING IN A LISBON MARKET

Alvaro is the son of a spice trader working in Lisbon, the capital of Portugal. He is 11 years old and works on his father's market stall. Alvaro and his friends recently joined the crowds welcoming home the explorer Vasco da Gama, who has returned from his Indian journey of 1497–1499. Spices have to be imported from the East, so Alvaro and his father hope more ships will travel to India and bring back produce they can sell.

Short tunic fastened with laces

Nutmeg

Cinnamon

Sugar loaf

Peppercorns

Blue hose, or stockings

Cardamom

Leather ankle boots

▶ Spice trader

Alvaro's father deals in spices, which grow in the Moluccas (or Spice Islands) and come to Portugal by land across Asia. They are expensive because they pass through Asia from one trader to another, each one making a profit.

Belém Tower, a defensive fortification completed in 1519

Lisbon

Lisbon is a major port and the world's largest trading centre. The wealth made from trade has brought a lot of money into the city and Portugal's ruler, King Manuel I, is having strong defences built to protect the harbour and the many ships anchored there.

1415
Portuguese Prince Henry the Navigator sends explorers into the Atlantic Ocean.

Prince Henry the Navigator

1488
Portuguese navigator Bartolomeu Dias explores the southern tip of Africa.

Age of exploration

In the 15th century, Portugal's sailors began to explore the coast of Africa, leaving settlers there to set up colonies. Explorers use the colonies as stopping places as they try to reach India and spice-growing islands such as the Moluccas.

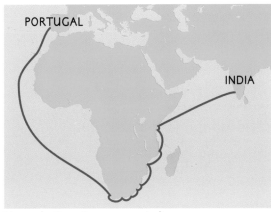

Vasco da Gama's voyage to India

Numeracy skills

Alvaro is very good with numbers. Working on the stall has given him lots of practice in adding up prices in his head. The Portuguese use a currency called the *real*, and their coins are made of gold or silver.

The *real*, Portuguese currency in the 15th century

Vasco da Gama

The Portuguese sailor Vasco da Gama is the first European to reach India by sea. When Alvaro sees da Gama return to Lisbon in 1499 he is greeted as a hero. The journey was dangerous but could mean that Portugal makes a lot more money.

Caravel

Caravels

The explorers' ships that Alvaro sees in Lisbon harbour are caravels. These are small ships usually about 12 to 18 m (40 to 60 ft) long, with triangular sails. These sails are perfect for navigating the changing winds of the Atlantic Ocean.

1492
Italian explorer Christopher Columbus sails across the Atlantic from Europe to the Caribbean.

Christopher Columbus

1497–1498
Vasco da Gama sails to India.

1511
Portuguese Afonso de Albuquerque conquers the Moluccas.

1519–1522
Portuguese sailor Ferdinand Magellan and his team sail all the way around the world.

1524
Vasco da Gama dies on his third Indian voyage.

Mariam

CHILD LIVING IN 16TH-CENTURY TIMBUKTU

Mariam is the ten-year-old daughter of a scholar living in Timbuktu during the early 1500s. Her home city is a centre of learning in Africa, with a large Islamic university that has many students and scholars. Timbuktu is a bustling city full of markets where merchants sell goods such as salt, ivory (elephant tusk), and books.

▼ City of learning

Outside the ancient university of Timbuktu are colourful markets packed with items to buy. Students pick up books copied from texts brought to the city by travellers. Mariam hopes to be a scholar when she is older, just like her dad.

Gold nugget

Gold currency

People in Timbuktu use gold nuggets as money. Gold pours into the city from mines in the nearby Bambouk Mountains.

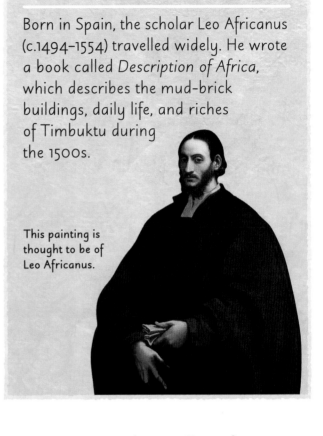

Djinguereber Mosque, part of the university

Tuaregs from the Sahara, carrying salt to trade

Slaves for sale at the market

Slabs of salt and cloth being sold

Scholars discussing a book

Spices for sale

Students carrying books

c.1200
Timbuktu grows as a trading centre for salt and gold.

Salt

c.1300
Sankore Mosque is first built – later it becomes part of Timbuktu's university.

c.1325
Timbuktu is made part of the Mali Empire by Mansa Musa.

Mansa Musa of Mali

1327
The Djinguereber Mosque is built.

Teaching tablets

It is important for Muslims to learn Arabic, so that they can read a religious book called the Qur'an. Mariam's brother goes to school at the local mosque. He learns the Qur'an off by heart by copying passages onto a wooden tablet.

Qur'anic tablet

Edge of the desert

Timbuktu is on the southern edge of the Sahara in west Africa, where the desert gives way to the Niger River valley. In 1500, it is at the heart of the Songhai Empire, and has a population of around 100,000, making it one of the world's biggest cities.

Key

Songhai Empire

SAHARA DESERT

Timbuktu

Niger River

Leather-bound book from the market that Mariam is carrying home for her father

Loose-fitting dress to keep cool in the intense heat

Pilgrims leaving for Mecca

Book stall

Scholar teaching the Qur'an

Boy herding goats

Fabric with a traditional West African pattern

1468
Timbuktu is taken over by the Songhai Empire of West Africa.

1493–1528
Songhai emperor Askia Muhammad I starts Timbuktu's golden age.

1591
Moroccan-paid soldiers conquer Songhai.

1593
Many scholars are accused of disloyalty and forced to leave.

Simona

CHILD IN FLORENCE DURING THE RENAISSANCE

Simona is 11 and lives in the city of Florence, Italy, in 1512. This is the time of the Renaissance, when the arts, sciences, architecture, and writing are incredibly popular. This period began in Italy when artists and writers rediscovered the culture of the ancient Greeks and Romans. Simona's family is wealthy and lives surrounded by beautiful things.

Detachable sleeve

White under-dress

Pearl necklace

Long, high-waisted dress

Florence

Florence is at the centre of the Renaissance. It is home to merchants and bankers who have the money to pay for building projects such as the cathedral's large dome, completed in 1436.

The invention of printing means that books are available.

Family coat of arms

Needlework is a favourite pastime for women.

Hand-carved furniture

1403
Lorenzo Ghiberti starts work on Florence Cathedral's baptistery doors.

Ghiberti's doors

1452
Leonardo da Vinci is born. He will become one of the most famous names of the Renaissance.

Visual arts

Oil painting is popular in the Renaissance. Artists paint and draw more realistically and study the form of the human body. One German artist, Albrecht Dürer, even wrote a book about human proportions (sizes).

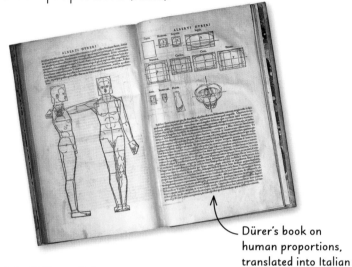

Dürer's book on human proportions, translated into Italian

▼ A life of luxury

Simona's father is a merchant and the family lives in a large house with well-made furniture, paintings on the walls, and servants. While her parents enjoy music and reading, the children have many handmade toys to play with, and dogs who follow them around.

Renaissance Italy

The Renaissance begins in the cities of Italy, especially Florence, Milan, and Rome. These cities are not only centres of business, they are also home to great artists, architects, and scholars.

Music

Most rich people in the Renaissance learn to read music. They love to sing, solo or in groups, and play instruments. Simona's mother is learning to play one of the most popular instruments, the lute.

Most lutes have 15 strings, which you pluck like a guitar.

A nursemaid takes care of the younger children.

Parts of the wall are painted with frescoes, a special painting technique.

Tapestry hangs on the living room wall

Family portrait

Maid

Children playing marbles

Hide and seek

1469
Banker Lorenzo de' Medici rules Florence, encouraging artists like Botticelli.

Small dogs were kept as pets, particularly by wealthy women.

1505–1512
Michelangelo paints Rome's Sistine Chapel.

1507
Artists such as Albrecht Dürer bring Renaissance ideas to northern Europe.

1529–1530
Spanish forces attack Florence; many artists go into hiding.

61

The Reformation

RELIGIOUS UPHEAVAL ACROSS EUROPE

In medieval Europe almost everyone went to church. As well as religious services, the Catholic Church provided people with education and healthcare. In the 16th century many people were worried that the Church wasn't being run properly. Some wanted to change the Church from within, and others to form new, Protestant churches. This movement was called the Reformation, and it had a huge impact on society.

Printing

The invention of printing meant that books, previously copied out by hand, could be reproduced quickly. This helped spread Reformation ideas. Translations of the Bible, previously mostly available only in Latin, were also printed. This meant everyone could understand its message.

Printing press

Luther demands change

A German monk, Martin Luther, was one of the best-known reformers. He opposed the practice of indulgences, where the Church offered a route to heaven for those who could pay. He allegedly posted a list of 95 arguments against indulgences on the church door at Wittenberg.

Closing the monasteries

King Henry VIII closed all the monasteries in England in the 1530s. Monasteries had provided education and charity. It took many years to set up new schools, so lots of children missed out on an education.

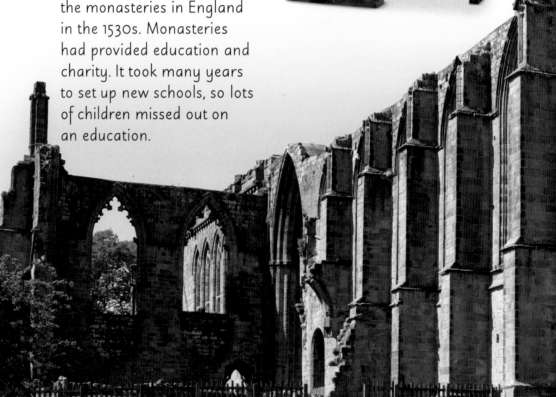

c.1439
German metalworker Johannes Gutenberg develops the printing press.

1517
Martin Luther protests against indulgences.

1524–1525
Peasants' War: German peasants rebel against Catholic power.

1527
The Reformation in Sweden begins under the influence of King Gustav I.

1534
England under Henry VIII breaks away from the Catholic Church.

Henry VIII

Europe in 1600

Key

- **Mainly Protestant**
- **Mainly Catholic**

Spread of reform

Campaigners like Martin Luther in Germany and John Calvin and Ulrich Zwingli in France and Switzerland began reform movements in their homelands. From here, Protestant reform spread to other places, including Scandinavia and Scotland.

Large dramatic statues of saints encouraged devotion during the Counter-Reformation.

The Church responds

The Catholic Church fought back with a movement called the Counter, or Catholic, Reformation. This involved a range of measures, from punishing those who opposed Church rules to more effective sermons and a new style of church art.

Bolton Abbey, one of the monasteries closed during the English Reformation

Thousands of Protestants were killed in the St Bartholomew's Day massacre.

Religious clashes

The 16th and 17th centuries saw much religious violence. In countries such as France, Protestants, including children, were murdered in the 1572 St Bartholomew's Day massacre. The bitter Thirty Years' War involved Protestant and Catholic forces across Europe.

1535
Protestants are punished in France. Many flee to other countries.

Protestants burned at the stake

1545
The Counter-Reformation begins.

1572
Many French Protestants are killed in the St Bartholomew's Day massacre.

1618–1648
The Thirty Years' War rages from Austria to Sweden.

63

Betim

JANISSARY IN THE OTTOMAN EMPIRE

Betim is an 11-year-old boy from Belgrade, Serbia. His city was conquered by the Ottoman Empire in 1521. Betim was captured and taken to a Turkish town, where he is training to be a member of the Janissaries, an elite fighting force that are effectively slaves of the Ottoman Sultan. Having joined the Janissaries, he has changed his religion to Islam and learned to speak Turkish.

Ottoman Empire

In 1520, the Ottoman Empire stretched across most of the Mediterranean region. The Ottoman leader, Suleiman I, soon expanded the empire even further, into north Africa, eastern Europe, and Iran.

Key

Ottoman Empire in 1520

Islam

The Ottomans are Muslims, followers of the religion of Islam. Muslims pray five times a day, often attending prayers at a local mosque. Under Islamic law only non-Muslims can be enslaved, so only non-Muslims like Betim can join the Janissaries.

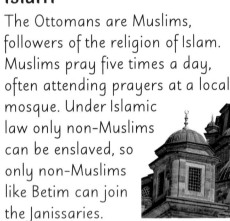

Mosque, Muslim worship place

Minaret, where the prayer call comes from

Wooden buildings

Coffee shop customers sitting on rugs and cushions

Janissaries making their way to the mosque

Water seller

Unloading a camel

1299
Osman I founds the Ottoman Empire in Anatolia (now Turkey).

Osman I

1362–1389
The empire expands into the Balkans in southeast Europe.

1380s
Recruitment of non-Muslim boys for the Janissary force begins.

1453
The Ottomans conquer Constantinople (now Istanbul) and make it their capital.

Battle of Mohács

Janissaries like Betim fight at the Battle of Mohács, Hungary, in 1526. When the Janissaries, armed with guns, defeat the Hungarians, a large part of Hungary comes under the control of the Ottoman Empire.

White linen turban

Kaftan

White undershirt beneath kaftan

Suleiman the Magnificent

As well as greatly expanding the empire, Suleiman I, known both as "the Magnificent" and "the Lawgiver", passed many new laws. He also paid for new palaces and mosques.

▼ Walking to the mosque

Hearing the call to prayer from one of the minarets, Betim makes his way to the mosque for prayers. He walks along streets of wooden houses, and passes busy shops and stalls.

Furniture-maker's shop

Janissary officers

Carpet seller

Carrying bread

Basket worker

Shalwar (loose trousers)

1520–1566
The empire grows even bigger under Suleiman the Magnificent.

1826
Mahmud II abolishes the Janissaries and sets up a modern army.

1922
With the founding of modern Turkey, the empire ceases to exist.

Edward VI

BOY KING OF ENGLAND

Edward VI became king when his father, King Henry VIII, died in 1547. Edward was only nine. England had been a Roman Catholic country, but in 1534 Henry VIII had declared that England would have its own Church. Later, Edward's advisers made the country fully Protestant. Religion played a big part in people's lives at the time, and many were upset by these changes.

Religious changes

In Edward's reign, Church leaders began having church services in English instead of the traditional Latin. Some extreme Protestants destroyed statues and paintings of saints and angels, as they saw them as overly Catholic.

Paintings of saints where their faces have been scratched out

Education

Edward was taught by the best scholars. He wrote clearly (left) and studied religion, philosophy, geometry, music, and languages. He was very good at languages, mastering Latin, Greek, French, Spanish, and Italian.

Studium meum ad te scribendi tantum est, ut quanquam me te breui uisurum sperem, tamen cum mihi sit otium uix queam mihi ipsi satis facere nisi ad te scripsero.   Non possum cum te non uehementer amare à qua sentio me plurimum diligi .   Amantissimus
tui Frater
Edouardus Princeps.

Family

Edward's mother was Henry VIII's third wife, Jane Seymour. She died soon after his birth. Henry longed for a son. He wanted his throne to pass to a male heir, because female rulers were thought to be weak.

Henry VIII

Jane Seymour

"I will see my laws strictly obeyed."
Edward VI to his sister, Mary Tudor

Kingdom

Edward ruled England and Wales. Scotland was a separate country at the time. Edward's advisers hoped to unite it with England by arranging for him to be married to the infant Mary, Queen of Scots.

SCOTLAND

ENGLAND

WALES

1536
Henry VIII marries Jane Seymour, hoping she will give him a son.

1537
Edward is born at Hampton Court Palace, just outside London.

Hampton Court Palace

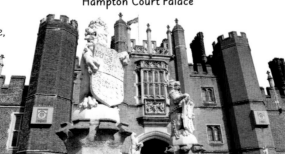

1541
Edward has a life-threatening fever, but recovers.

1543
Edward is engaged to the seven-month-old Mary, Queen of Scots.

1547
Henry VIII dies, and Edward VI becomes king.

1548
England and Scotland are at war. Mary is sent to France, where she will marry the French king's son.

1549
Economic problems result in riots and rebellions in England.

1553
Edward dies at Greenwich Palace of an unknown illness. His sister Mary, a Catholic, becomes queen.

Mary I of England

Pocahontas

POWHATAN GIRL WHO BECAME A LEGEND

Pocahontas was the daughter of a chief of the Powhatan, a Native American tribe from the Tidewater area of Virginia. When she was about 12 years old, she is said to have saved the life of John Smith, the English leader of Jamestown. Later she married the English settler John Rolfe, and travelled to England. She became famous as a Native American who lived in peace with the English.

Saving John Smith

John Smith said that Pocahontas's father was going to behead him, but Pocahontas saved his life. Whether or not this actually happened is debated by historians.

Jamestown

Jamestown, founded in 1607, was the first permanent English settlement in North America. The settlers chose the site because they could defend it easily and local Powhatans did not use it.

Jamestown •

> **"She laid her own [head] upon his to save him from death."**
> *Captain John Smith*

Life in London

When she lived in London, Pocahontas wore English clothes and was viewed as an example of a "civilized" person from a different culture. She became famous, but died aged about 21 before she could return to America.

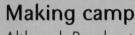

Making camp

Although Pocahontas was a chief's daughter, she would have lived like the rest of the Powhatan people, in a simple wigwam. She spent her time learning to build fires, cook, and gather food.

Wigwam covered with birch-tree bark and woven matting

A portrait of Pocahontas made while she was in London

1596
Pocahontas is born to chief Powhatan and one of his wives.

1607
Captain John Smith and other English settlers arrive in Virginia.

John Smith's map of Virginia

1607–1608
Smith is captured and Pocahontas is said to have saved his life.

1609
War breaks out between the English and Powhatan people.

1610
It is said that Pocahontas marries Kocoum, of the Patawomeck tribe.

Chief's daughter

Pocahontas's father was a chief, so she would have worn fine clothes and shell beads to show that she came from an important family.

1613
Pocahontas is captured by the English and Kocoum is killed.

1614
Pocahontas marries Englishman John Rolfe and becomes a Christian.

Pocahontas's baptism

January 1615
Pocahontas gives birth to a son, Thomas Rolfe.

1616
The Rolfe family travels to England.

1617
Pocahontas becomes ill and dies in Gravesend, England.

Akachi

AFRICAN BOY ENSLAVED IN VIRGINIA

Akachi was born in west Africa, but in 1660, when he was ten, he was sent to North America to work as a slave. He survived the gruelling two-month journey across the Atlantic and has worked in Virginia for about a year. In America his owner renamed him Jack. Some slaves become household servants, but Akachi works on a large farm, called a plantation. The work is hard and for slaves there is no chance of escape, no free time, and no money.

Slave auction

As soon as a slave ship arrives in America, the slaves are sold at auction. American colonists want to buy healthy-looking slaves, and families are often split up when buyers want only young, strong workers.

Triangular trade

The slave's journey is one part of a three-way route. Ships exchange slaves for crops in America, which are then taken to Europe. From there, goods, such as textiles and guns, are taken to Africa to be traded for more slaves.

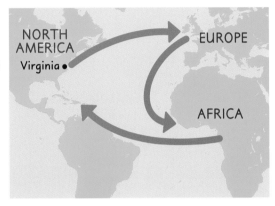

Slave ship

On the two-month voyage the slaves are crammed so close together they can hardly move. The ship is dirty and slaves are beaten if they complain. Many don't survive the journey.

Low ceilings force slaves to lie down

Men were often chained together for the journey.

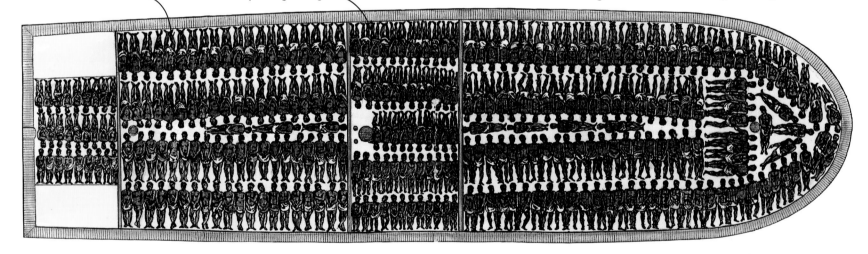

1501
Spanish settlers bring the first African slaves to the Caribbean.

1612
Tobacco is first grown for sale in Jamestown, Virginia.

Tobacco is smoked in long, wooden pipes.

1619
Britain's North American colonies import slaves for the first time.

1663
First recorded slave rebellion takes place in Gloucester County, Virginia.

Plantations

In North American colonies, such as Virginia, and in colonies in the Caribbean, settlers grow crops like sugar and tobacco on large plantations. Using slaves like Akachi means plantation owners have low labour costs and make lots of money selling their produce.

Clothes are cheap, threadbare, and ill-fitting.

Hoe with wooden handle

Short breeches made of woollen fabric

Cotton bandage covers injury

Punishment

The overseer, a white man who works for the plantation owner, watches the slaves all the time. He beats or whips anyone who does not work hard, or brands them with a red-hot iron.

An overseer threatens the whip to make everyone work harder.

◀ Working the fields

Every day, Akachi works long hours from dawn to dusk, with only simple hand tools like hoes and spades. It is a very tough life and slaves aren't expected to live very long.

1777
Vermont becomes the first colony to abolish slavery.

1808
The USA bans the importing of African slaves.

President Abraham Lincoln signed the 13th Amendment.

1865
The 13th Amendment to the US Constitution outlaws slavery.

John

CABIN BOY ON A PIRATE SHIP

John is 12 years old. He is a cabin boy on an English pirate ship sailing around the Caribbean Sea in the year 1702. Until six months ago he worked on a ship transporting goods, but pirates attacked it and took him prisoner. Now he works for the pirates, doing everything from cooking to carrying dangerous gunpowder to the guns when the pirates want to attack another ship.

Plundering paradise

The pirates mostly attack ships that belong to Spain, England's enemy. The crew are on the lookout for things they can sell or use, such as gold and silver coins, weapons, tools, rope, and goods such as sugar and rum.

Red jacket over plain cotton shirt

Pirate captain watching a ship on the horizon

▼ Daily chores

John's work includes keeping the deck clean and acting as a servant to the captain and crew members. He also climbs the rigging to help adjust the sails.

Musicians keep the pirates entertained.

The Jolly Roger flag is only raised during an attack.

Loose short trousers called "slops"

1492
Christopher Columbus first brings European ships to the Caribbean.

16th century
The Spanish export silver from Bolivia and Mexico, attracting pirates.

Wooden bucket for carrying water

Goods are stored in barrels.

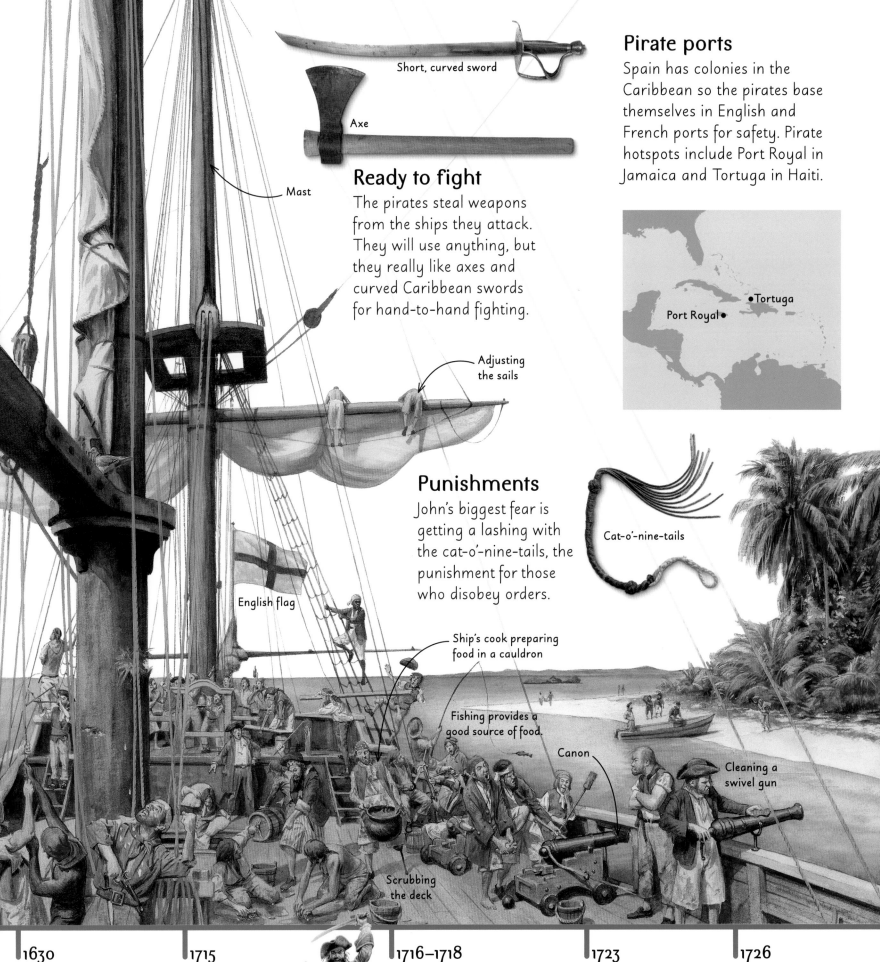

Short, curved sword

Axe

Mast

Ready to fight

The pirates steal weapons
from the ships they attack.
They will use anything, but
they really like axes and
curved Caribbean swords
for hand-to-hand fighting.

Pirate ports

Spain has colonies in the
Caribbean so the pirates base
themselves in English and
French ports for safety. Pirate
hotspots include Port Royal in
Jamaica and Tortuga in Haiti.

•Tortuga

Port Royal•

Adjusting
the sails

Punishments

John's biggest fear is
getting a lashing with
the cat-o'-nine-tails, the
punishment for those
who disobey orders.

Cat-o'-nine-tails

English flag

Ship's cook preparing
food in a cauldron

Fishing provides a
good source of food.

Canon

Cleaning a
swivel gun

Scrubbing
the deck

1630
Pirates base themselves
on Tortuga in Haiti,
home to French and
English settlers.

1715
Nassau in
the Bahamas
becomes the
last pirate port.

1716–1718
Edward Teach ("Blackbeard")
takes ships in South
Carolina, North America,
before being killed.

1723
Stronger navies start
to control piracy.

1726
The "Golden Age of
Piracy", when piracy
is at its peak, ends.

Blackbeard

Mozart

Real life

CHILD MUSICAL PRODIGY

Wolfgang Amadeus Mozart was one of the greatest of all classical composers. Born in Salzburg, Austria, he was already learning to play the piano at three years old, and was writing his own music by the time he was five. He amazed audiences as a child and continued to impress them by composing more than 600 pieces of music before he died at 35.

European tour

Mozart travelled a lot, putting on operas in cities such as Prague. He also played concerts in Paris, Munich, and Vienna, where he lived for the last years of his life.

Piano master

Some of Mozart's greatest pieces were written for the piano. As an adult, Mozart organized concerts in which he played music he had composed himself. He was an excellent performer.

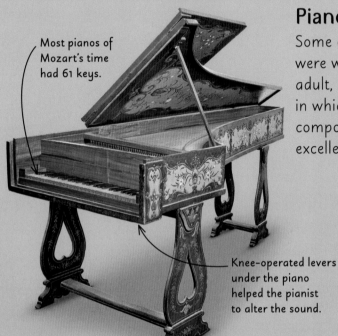

Most pianos of Mozart's time had 61 keys.

Knee-operated levers under the piano helped the pianist to alter the sound.

> "Your son is the greatest composer known to me either in person or by name."
>
> Josef Haydn, 1785

Early pieces

Mozart was composing short dance pieces for the piano by the time he was five. In his teens, he wrote many symphonies, violin compositions, and choral pieces, which were praised by audiences.

Opera legacy

Mozart's operas are still incredibly popular today. Among the greatest are *The Marriage of Figaro* and *The Magic Flute*, with its funny character, the bird-catcher Papageno.

1756
Wolfgang Amadeus Mozart is born in Salzburg, Austria.

1762
Mozart goes on a European tour as a child prodigy.

Archbishop of Salzburg

1773–1781
Mozart works as a musician for the Archbishop of Salzburg.

1781
Mozart settles in Vienna, where he writes many of his best known works.

1782
Mozart marries Constanze Weber in Vienna.

Family time

As a boy, Mozart gave piano concerts with his talented sister, Nannerl, and his father, Leopold, who was a composer and violinist.

1782–1785
Mozart plays his own piano concertos in a series of concerts in Vienna.

Programme for *The Marriage of Figaro*'s first performance

1786
The Marriage of Figaro premieres.

1789–1790
Short of money, Mozart plays lots of concerts in Germany.

1791
Mozart writes *The Magic Flute*.

5 December 1791
Mozart dies in Vienna, Austria, of an unknown illness.

Kaha'i

MASTER BOAT-BUILDER'S APPRENTICE IN HAWAII

Kaha'i is ten years old and lives on the island of Hawaii in the 18th century, when the islands will soon be visited by the British explorer James Cook. Kaha'i is an apprentice to a master canoe-maker, and is learning to shape wood using traditional tools such as the stone-bladed *adze*. This is an important craft as island people need canoes to get from island to island.

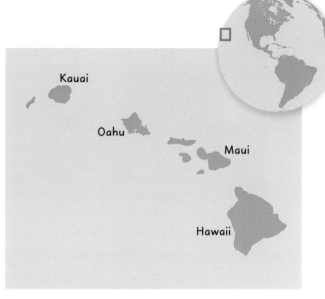

Kauai

Oahu

Maui

Hawaii

Hawaiian islands

Hawaii is a group of islands that lies in the middle of the Pacific Ocean. Kaha'i lives on the largest island, which is also called Hawaii. The first settlers probably came in canoes from Polynesian islands to the south. They brought with them plants such as taro, which they grew for food.

The god Lono was said to bring rain to make the ground good for growing plants.

Hull carved from a single piece of loa wood

Outrigger

Lono

The Hawaiian god of farming, rain, and peace is called Lono. In myths, he existed before the creation of the Earth and is said to reappear as a human. Some Hawaiian people thought that the European explorer Captain Cook was Lono in human form.

Outrigger canoe

Small Hawaiian canoes have a hull carved from a single tree trunk. They also have an outrigger, which helps to keep the canoe stable in the rough seas and windy conditions around the islands.

c.300–1200 CE
People from Polynesia begin to settle in Hawaii.

1778–1779
Navigator James Cook is the first European to visit Hawaii.

1780
The Hawaiian population begins to fall because of disease.

1795
Kamehameha I starts the royal dynasty that will rule for most of the 19th century.

1875
Sugar production increases because of a treaty with the USA.

Sugar cane

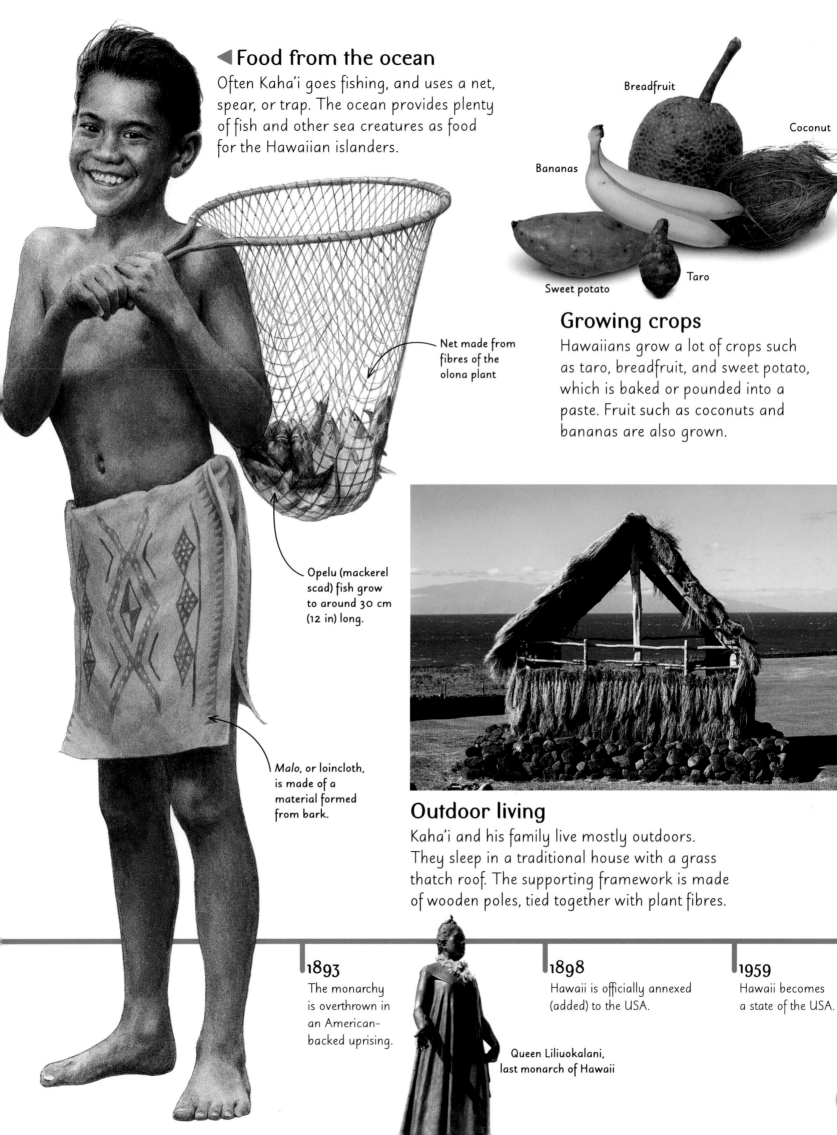

◄ Food from the ocean

Often Kaha'i goes fishing, and uses a net, spear, or trap. The ocean provides plenty of fish and other sea creatures as food for the Hawaiian islanders.

Breadfruit

Coconut

Bananas

Sweet potato

Taro

Net made from fibres of the olona plant

Growing crops

Hawaiians grow a lot of crops such as taro, breadfruit, and sweet potato, which is baked or pounded into a paste. Fruit such as coconuts and bananas are also grown.

Opelu (mackerel scad) fish grow to around 30 cm (12 in) long.

Malo, or loincloth, is made of a material formed from bark.

Outdoor living

Kaha'i and his family live mostly outdoors. They sleep in a traditional house with a grass thatch roof. The supporting framework is made of wooden poles, tied together with plant fibres.

1893
The monarchy is overthrown in an American-backed uprising.

Queen Liliuokalani, last monarch of Hawaii

1898
Hawaii is officially annexed (added) to the USA.

1959
Hawaii becomes a state of the USA.

School through time

A JOURNEY THROUGH THE HISTORY OF EDUCATION

For much of human history, few children went to school. Those who did were mostly boys with rich parents, or those who would need to read and write for their work. Teachers mostly taught reading, writing, and maths. The 19th century saw an increase in the number of girls and poorer children going to school, as well as the variety of subjects taught.

Egyptian scribes used reed pens.

Egyptian hieroglyphic script was intentionally difficult, so only scribes could read it.

Ancient Egypt

The Egyptians had elite schools where rich boys learned to be scribes, people who copied documents and kept records. They used hundreds of symbols called hieroglyphs.

Writing on a clay tablet

Ancient Babylon

In ancient Babylon, pupils sat in rows on wooden benches and learned how to write letters and legal documents. They wrote on tablets of soft clay, and in Babylon the school was called the "tablet house".

The Torah was written on parchment scrolls like those found in synagogues today.

Ancient Israel

In ancient Israel, children learned to read in order to understand religious texts, especially the Torah (Hebrew Bible) and Talmud (commentary on the Torah).

Teachers started using blackboards to display information.

The Middle Ages

Few children in the medieval period (400–1400) went to school. Those who did learned Latin, the language used by scholars and priests all over Europe. The children memorized words and phrases by reciting them out loud.

20th century

In the 20th century, children in many countries had to go to school by law. Sat at desks, pupils learned by listening to the teacher before working on their own or in groups.

17th century

More people went to school in the 17th century, especially in towns and cities. Printed books helped pupils learn about religion, natural history, and geography.

Modern classroom

Today classrooms are more hi-tech, with computers and tablets making learning exciting. The Internet is helping to bring education to children who live in isolated parts of the world.

Illustrated books for children did not appear until the 17th century.

The American Revolution

AMERICANS FIGHT TO RULE

The American Revolution (1775–1781) was a struggle between the American colonists and their British rulers. Many young people were involved in the war. The colonists won and formed the United States of America.

Coffins bearing the initials of casualties of the Boston Massacre

Spark of the revolution

In 1770, a British supporter killed an 11-year-old boy in Boston. Soon after, British soldiers shot dead people protesting against British taxes. Known as the Boston Massacre, this sparked more protests and led to war.

Lexington, 1775

Boston

Trenton, 1776

Battle sites

The first battle of the war took place at Lexington on 18 April 1775. The British were defeated. Fighting spread south to Virginia and north to New Hampshire.

Fighting for the colonists

The colonists' forces – both the local militia forces and the more organised Continental Army – included boys aged 15 or younger. Children as young as seven served as messengers, spies, and drummers.

Captain John Parker, leader of the Lexington militia

5 March 1770
British troops kill protesters in the Boston Massacre.

16 December 1773
People throw tea into Boston harbour to protest against paying high taxes.

Colonists, dressed as Native Americans, throwing tea into Boston harbour

19 April 1775
The Battle of Lexington marks the start of the war.

17 June 1775
The Battle of Bunker Hill is won by the British, but many British soldiers die.

Life on the home front

With so many boys joining the army, girls had to do more work. Some grew vegetables to provide food. Others spun wool, wove cloth, or made much-needed clothes for the soldiers. Many girls also did housework while their mothers went out to work.

Declaration of Independence

In 1776, the colonists announced their independence from the British Empire in the famous Declaration, signed by leaders such as Thomas Jefferson and Benjamin Franklin. It stated that "all men are created equal".

Declaration of Independence, written by Thomas Jefferson

An early version of the Stars and Stripes with 13 stars representing the original colonies.

Turning point

In December 1776, George Washington and his army crossed the Delaware River, launching a surprise attack on the British at Trenton. Other successes followed. The colonists eventually won the war in 1781.

4 July 1776
The Declaration of Independence is put in place by the colonists.

25 December 1776
George Washington crosses the Delaware River.

January 1781
The colonists' victory at Cowpens stops British progressing further south.

Continental Army hat

19 October 1781
The war ends with the colonists' victory at Yorktown.

1783
Britain signs the Treaty of Paris, officially recognising the USA.

Modern period

CHAPTER FIVE

This period stretches from the 1780s to today. It has seen a huge growth in the number of people on Earth, the rise of industry and factory work, several devastating wars, and the banning of slavery in most countries. Many families have a comfortable life and good education, but there is still much poverty around the world.

Jean-François

CHILD OF THE FRENCH REVOLUTION

Ten-year-old Jean-François is growing up in Paris in 1790. He works with his father, who is a tailor. It is the time of the revolution, when people are trying to change the way France is ruled. They believe the king, the aristocracy, and the Church have too much power. Jean-François' family, like many people, are poor and hungry.

Revolutionary France

The revolution started near the French capital, Paris, but poor peasants in the countryside also supported the protest. In 1793, a three-year war in the Vendée region broke out between those who were for and against the revolution.

Royalty and poverty

The king and queen have one of the most luxurious courts in Europe, with a palace at Versailles, expensive clothes, jewellery, and hundreds of servants. Their lives are very different from the poverty suffered by most people.

▶ Supporting change

Jean-François and his father support the revolutionary group *sans-culottes*. They want the king to have less power, new, fairer laws, and proper human rights for all French people.

Queen Marie Antoinette

King Louis XVI

Red Phrygian cap is a symbol of the revolution

Tricolour French flag, first used during the revolution

Tricolour cockade is the badge of the revolution

Sans-culottes means "without breeches". The supporters wear loose trousers, instead of the tight breeches of the upper classes.

Worker's wooden-soled, leather shoes

1789
A mob storms the Bastille prison in Paris, starting the revolution.

10 August 1792
Revolutionaries enter the Tuileries Palace and imprison the royal family.

Bread

Mushrooms

Lack of food

Food shortages due to droughts and cold weather have led to widespread famine. Even bread is expensive because bad grain harvests have pushed up prices. Some people grow mushrooms in cellars for them to eat. Others are so desperate that they steal food to survive.

Tailor's workshop

Tailor's apprentice

Jean-François is an apprentice in a large tailor's workshop. He learns how to mark out cloth using chalk, how to cut it correctly, and the different stitches used to sew garments. Tailors usually have plenty of work, but Jean-François and his family do not have much food, because of the shortages.

Shears for cutting cloth

Bastille prison, Paris

Fighting begins

The revolution began when a group attacked the royal Bastille prison in Paris, released prisoners, and took weapons stored there. Later the revolution became violent, with fighting in some parts of France. In Paris, thousands of opponents of the revolution, including the king and queen, are executed by beheading at the guillotine.

September 1792
The First Republic is set up to replace the monarchy.

21 January 1793
Louis XVI is executed in Paris.

Guillotine used for executions

1793–1794
With the revolution under threat, 20,000 people are executed by the government.

1799
A group of conspirators, including Napoleon Bonaparte, overthrow the government.

1804
Napoleon becomes emperor of France, ending the First Republic.

Marie Antoinette

Real life ★

QUEEN OF FRANCE

Marie Antoinette, daughter of Francis and Maria-Theresa, Emperor and Empress of Austria, was born in 1755. She was raised in palaces in Vienna but did not see her parents much – her father died in 1765 and her mother was often busy. At 14, she moved to Paris to be the wife of Prince Louis, the future king of France. The French did not like her extravagant ways, and she was executed during the French Revolution.

Music

Upper-class girls in the 18th century were made to learn skills, such as dancing and playing music, that would be useful at fancy parties. Marie Antoinette was a good dancer and liked to sing. At her first public appearance, aged three, she sang a song for her father's birthday.

As a child, Marie Antoinette learned to play the harp and the piano.

In Paris

Marie Antoinette was often sad in Paris, so far from her home in Vienna. She hardly knew her husband, and she spoke the French language poorly. The locals and the people at court were not kind to her either.

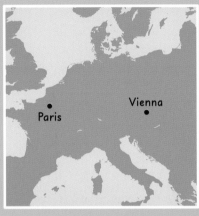

Paris • Vienna •

> "I am calm, as one may well be when one's conscience is clear..."
>
> Marie Antoinette's final letter

Marie Antoinette awaits execution

Portrait of Louis before he became king

Louis XVI

France was gearing up for revolution when Louis became king. The French people believed that taxes were too high and that the king had too much power. Louis, however, believed the king's power was God-given and was not to be questioned.

The French Revolution

In 1789, the fight over how France should be ruled began. The revolutionaries, people who wanted to get rid of the monarchy, won. Marie Antoinette and Louis were executed, and the people of France took control of their country.

1755
Princess Maria Antonia Josepha Joanna, known as Marie Antoinette, is born at Hofburg Palace.

Hofburg Palace in Vienna, Austria

1770
Marie Antoinette marries Louis-Auguste, heir to the French throne.

1774
Louis is crowned King Louis XVI of France, and Marie Antoinette becomes queen.

1778
Marie-Thérèse Charlotte, Marie Antoinette's first child, is born.

Image of elegance
When Marie Antoinette and Louis were to be married, the prince sent a painter to Vienna to paint her so he could see how his bride-to-be looked.

1781
The queen is accused of stealing and sending money from France to her family in Austria.

1785
A group of jewellers accuses the queen of a crime involving a diamond necklace.

1789
The royal family is placed under house arrest in Paris.

1792
The French monarchy is abolished.

Louis XVI and Marie Antoinette with their family before execution

1793
Marie Antoinette and Louis XVI are executed in Paris.

Mary

CHILD WORKING IN A COTTON MILL

Mary Roberts is a ten-year-old girl from a town near Manchester in England. In 1797, when she was seven, both of her parents died and she became homeless. She was sent to a cotton mill, where she has to work until she is 21. In return she gets food, somewhere to stay, and a very low wage.

Basket for collecting cotton waste

Plain cotton dress

Cotton apron

Water-powered

The mill is full of machines called spinning mules, which turn cotton into thread that can be woven into cloth. The power that runs the machines comes from a fast-flowing river that turns a huge water wheel.

Piecer mending broken thread

Machine operator

Spinning mule

Rows of spindles

1709 onwards
Improvements in iron-making make the metal cheaper and more plentiful.

1712
Thomas Newcomen produces the first successful steam engine.

1775–1779
Samuel Crompton develops the spinning mule.

1803
Samuel Horrocks's power loom speeds up weaving.

Few pauper children owned shoes.

Industrial Revolution

The move from doing work by hand to using machines happens quickly across northern Europe. Thousands of people like Mary are working in the new factories. This change is called the Industrial Revolution.

• Manchester

▼ Dangerous work

Mary works as a scavenger, picking up bits of cotton from the floor, so that they are not wasted. She has to take care not to get hurt when climbing under the machines.

Potatoes

Milk

Oatcakes

Porridge oats

Simple food

The mill owner only gives Mary and the other children the cheapest food and does not even provide enough cutlery for everyone. Mary drinks milk and mainly eats potatoes, oatcakes, and porridge made with oats and water.

Housing for workers

Mary lives in the mill's apprentice house. There is very little room – about 90 children are crammed into the house. Homeless children like Mary are called pauper apprentices.

Watching the machine for broken threads

Overseer making sure everyone is working hard

Boy comforting another child with an injured hand

Scavenger collecting cotton from under the machine

Mill owner

Boy sweeping

Pushing a basket of cotton

Spindles of spun thread

1807 onwards
Many factories and ironworks are built in Belgium.

1815
Factories powered by steam engines become common.

1815 onwards
Many mines, factories, and ironworks open in Germany's Ruhr district.

1825 onwards
Railways help with the transportation of goods and raw materials.

Steam locomotive for industrial transport

Maratinyeri

ABORIGINAL BOY FROM THE LOWER MURRAY RIVER

Maratinyeri is a ten-year-old boy who lives by the Lower Murray River, South Australia, in the 19th century. His family are Australian Aborigines of the Ngarrindjeri people. Each year, Maratinyeri moves with his group between their summer and winter camps to take advantage of the foods available at different seasons. He knows the land well, and it has a deep religious significance for his people.

Armband made from reed

Taro, an edible plant

Rush-fibre belt holds loincloth in place

Kangaroo-skin loincloth

Rush-fibre basket containing bulrush roots

Murray River

Life by the river

There are many Aboriginal groups living near the Murray River. Maratinyeri's people live by the lower river, near the coast. They never need to move too far because the land is fertile and the river is full of fish and shellfish.

◀ Gathering bulrushes

Maratinyeri gathers bulrushes, reed-like plants, that grow in the creeks. These are useful for making baskets, clothes, and fishing nets. He chews the bulrushes, and then rubs the fibres against his thigh to twist them into a twine. He uses this twine to make things.

1700
Several hundred thousand Aboriginal people live in Australia.

1770
James Cook claims the east coast of Australia for Britain.

James Cook

1789
Aboriginal people in New South Wales suffer from smallpox for the first time.

On the hunt

Maratinyeri's father and elder brothers fish in the river, spear wildfowl, and hunt animals such as kangaroos. They kill the animals with stone-tipped spears, or catch them in nets hung between trees or across creeks.

Murray River

The lower river is wide and has plenty of fish. It floods in springtime, filling up the nearby swamps and backwater lakes, or "billabongs". When the floods come, Maratinyeri and his family move to an island among the swamps.

Food supplies

Maratinyeri's mother and sisters catch crayfish in the river and dive into the water to gather mussels. They also gather berries and grubs. These are added to the bulrush roots, which the family mainly eats for meals.

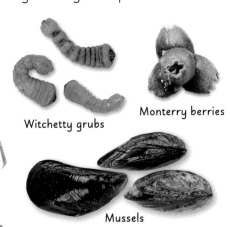

Witchetty grubs

Monterry berries

Mussels

Crayfish

Faithful friend

The dingo, or Australian wild dog, is a valued companion for Maratinyeri's people. Dogs join the men on hunting expeditions, guard the camp against strangers or predators, and sleep next to the people at night, helping to keep them warm.

1795
First battle between the British and Aboriginal people, who are defending their land.

Boomerangs used as weapons

1810
Europeans move Aboriginal people to "mission stations" to learn European beliefs.

1905
The Australian government removes children from many Aboriginal families.

1920s
Aboriginal population is under 90,000, with a lot of Aboriginal people living away from their lands.

Nayra

GIRL IN NEWLY INDEPENDENT BOLIVIA

Nayra is a ten-year-old girl living in the high-up Altiplano region of Bolivia in 1830. Her country has only just become independent from the Spanish, who ruled it for centuries. Nayra lives in a small village, where her family are farmers who grow potatoes and look after a herd of woolly alpacas and llamas. They take their herds to the lush grass on the lower mountain slopes in the summer, and bring them back to the village in the winter.

Colourfully patterned *lluchu* wool hat

Baby alpaca, used for wool and milk when it grows up

Alpaca wool

Nayra and her mother spin thread from alpaca wool. This is dyed in bright colours and the women of the village weave it into cloth. All of Nayra's clothes are made of hand-woven cloth.

Rectangular cloth *aguayo* is knotted to carry things in

Plain leading to snow-capped mountains

Boy leading alpaca

Herd of alpacas

1530s
Francisco Pizarro conquers Bolivia and its neighbours for Spain.

Statue of Pizarro

1824
Spanish royalist forces are defeated, securing independence for South America.

1825
Bolivia is named after Bolívar, who is president of the new country.

New borders

The Spanish rulers called Nayra's homeland Upper Peru. Now independent, the new country of Bolivia has boundaries with Brazil in the east and Chile in the west.

BOLIVIA

Altiplano

Simón Bolívar

Bolívar is the political and military leader who led the struggle against South America's Spanish rulers. He has become a hero for many, and the people of Nayra's area decide to call their new country after him.

Each pipe sounds a different note when the *siku* is blown at the top.

Making music

Nayra loves the music of the *siku*, a wind instrument. She and her aunts play their *sikus* with other women from the village during summer in the lower mountains.

▼ Mountain village

Nayra's family live in a small mud-brick house with a thatched roof. It gets quite cold up in the mountains, so Nayra wears thick woollen clothing and several petticoats under her skirt.

Man sorting potatoes into a basket

Woman harvesting potatoes

Man mending a thatched roof

Woman carrying her baby in an *aguayo*

Mud-walled house with thatched roof

Weaving on a hand loom

Grain being ground

1840
Bolivia declines in wealth and influence in South America.

1879–1883
Bolivia loses some land to Chile in the War of the Pacific.

c.1890
Tin-mining makes the country richer, though miners are poorly paid.

1920
Rebellion by indigenous (native) Bolivians, who can't vote.

1952
Bolivian revolution gives all adults the vote.

Tin from a mine

Pedro II

EMPEROR OF BRAZIL

Pedro II was a much-loved ruler of Brazil in the 19th century. When Pedro was six, his father, Pedro I, gave up his throne to go to Portugal and help his daughter secure her rule there. Pedro II took up his duties as emperor when he came of age at 15, and ruled for nearly 50 years. He proved to be a popular monarch, keeping his large country stable, building its power in South America, and encouraging education, the arts, and the sciences.

Father's second marriage
Pedro was only one when his mother died. His father then married Princess Amélie of Leuchtenberg, whom Pedro who fond of. The couple left Brazil five years later, leaving Pedro behind to one day rule as emperor.

Palace life
As a child, Pedro hardly ever left the royal palace. He was made to spend most of his time studying. He got on well with his sisters, but he was only allowed a little time with them each day.

Camera from the 19th century

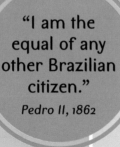

"I am the equal of any other Brazilian citizen."
Pedro II, 1862

BRAZIL

Rio de Janeiro

Leading Brazil
When Pedro took over from the men appointed to rule on his behalf, he was welcomed as a figure of authority. He worked with politicians, helping them to come to agreements. He also encouraged developments such as railways that made travelling around the country easier.

Eager to learn
Pedro read widely in subjects from medicine and science to philosophy and law. He spoke over 12 languages and promoted arts and education. Always interested in new ideas and technology, Pedro was the first person in Brazil to own a camera.

1825
Dom Pedro de Alcântara is born in Rio de Janeiro.

1826
Pedro's mother dies. His father, Pedro I, remarries in 1829.

1831
Pedro I gives up the throne. Pedro II's advisers rule Brazil until he comes of age at 15.

1841
Pedro is crowned emperor in his own right.

1843
Pedro marries Teresa Cristina, an Italian princess.

Bust of Pedro II in Rio de Janeiro

Young emperor

Although young Pedro was shy and uncertain of himself, he became a successful ruler who was well liked by his people.

1852
Brazil and its allies defeat Argentina in the Platine War.

1867
Pedro makes a speech calling for the end of slavery.

Pedro II giving a speech to his government

1888
Slavery is finally ended in Brazil.

1889
Pedro stands down as emperor after a military uprising.

1891
Pedro dies in Paris, France.

Martha

CHILD TRAVELLING THROUGH THE WILD WEST

Ten-year-old Martha Grant was born in the USA, in a small town in Missouri. In 1845, her parents decided to join other families heading west to find new land to farm. Life is tough on the trail. The wagons are filled with belongings, so the travellers have to walk all day through country they don't know. There is no school for Martha – she has to help her mother with chores.

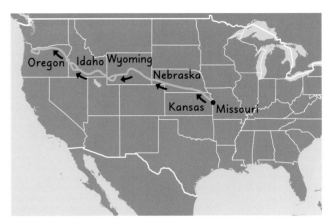

Trading with locals

Martha's family meets Native Americans on the journey. Mostly the locals and travellers are friendly with each other. They trade together and Martha gets a pair of buffalo-skin moccasins.

Moccasins made from buffalo skin

The Oregon Trail

The route through the "Wild West" is called the Oregon Trail and it passes through the modern states of Missouri, Kansas, Nebraska, Wyoming, Idaho, and Oregon. It takes nearly six months to walk the 3,492-km (2,170-mile) trail.

▼ Camping for the night

The families stop for the night near a small lake in Wyoming, pitch their tents, and cook their meals. Ahead, they can see the Rocky Mountains, where the trail will get steeper and more difficult.

Rods support the wagons.

Playing instruments for entertainment

Families pitching tents

Fort where goods could be traded

Trail guide planning route

Cooking over an open fire

Reading the Bible to children

Possessions stored inside the wagons

Washing clothes

Chopping wood for the fire

Fitting wagon wheels

1811
Fur traders found Fort Astoria, the first white settlement in Oregon.

1843
The first group of wagons reaches the western part of the Oregon Trail.

1845
The building of the Barlow Road makes the western part of the trail easier.

1848
Gold is discovered near Coloma, California, bringing people west.

Gold nugget

1862
The Homestead Act gives families the right to settle freely on the Great Plains.

Hair tied back
with a bow

Grubby
cotton
collar

Home-sewn
rag doll

Herding cattle

Travellers bring with them
a small herd of six to ten
cattle, plus a cow or two
for milking. Cattle provide
meat if they can find no buffalo
or antelope to shoot on the way.
The children help their fathers
lead the cattle as they travel.

Life on the road

Martha helps her mother
cook food and wash clothes.
Washing by hand involves
dunking the clothes in a
tub of hot, soapy water
and rubbing them against
a metal washboard to
remove dirt.

Martha wears a
simple cotton apron
when doing chores.

Water is collected
from the river.

Trading
with Native
Americans

The Rocky Mountains

Abandoned
wagon

Cattle

Searching for
game to shoot

Tough leather
boots, perfect for
walking across
grassland

1865
The US Civil War
ends and many
former soldiers
settle in the west.

1884
A rail link between
Oregon and the Midwest
effectively ends the
Oregon Trail.

Union Pacific Railroad

Transport through time

A JOURNEY THROUGH THE HISTORY OF TRAVEL

The way people get around has changed a lot over the centuries. Often an invention takes years to spread across the world. Forms of transport such as cars and aeroplanes started out as luxuries for the rich before they caught on more widely, transforming the lives of millions.

Large, square sails made of woollen cloth

Stone Age

Towards the end of the Stone Age, around 4800 BCE, people in central Asia began to herd and tame horses for riding. Early domesticated horses may have been similar to the wild Przewalski's horse of Mongolia.

Vikings

From the Stone Age to Viking times and beyond, wooden boats were widely used to travel along rivers and across seas. The Greeks, Romans, and Vikings used ships with both sails and oars. Viking ships were well built and fast, and could be used for surprise coastal attacks.

Carts were used for goods, while people walked or rode horses.

Medieval period

By the medieval period (400–1400) farmers and merchants were using wheeled carts, pulled by horses or oxen, to carry farm goods, such as hay. Rough, bumpy roads and tracks meant the wooden wheels and axles often needed repairing.

19th century

Trains hauled by steam engines appeared in the early 19th century. George Stephenson's *Rocket* was one of the first engines. It only travelled at 45 kph (28 mph), but soon other trains appeared that were much faster, making long-distance travel possible.

Modern transport

Climate change means it is important we develop transport that doesn't pollute the environment. Electric cars have batteries you can charge at home. With electricity generated from renewable sources, like wind or solar power, this offers a green alternative to oil as a fuel.

The Comet was the first airliner to have a turbojet engine.

Early 20th century

Although cars started to be made in the 1880s, the first one to reach a big market was the Model T Ford. It came out in 1908, and was cheap, rugged, and easy to repair. Around 14 million of these cars were sold.

Late 20th century

When the first tiny aeroplanes took off at the start of the 20th century, no one thought that by the 1950s there would be jet airliners like the de Havilland Comet. They carried 80 people at up to 840 kph (520 mph), making international travel available to everyone.

Seamus

IRISH IMMIGRANT IN NEW YORK CITY

Seamus was born in a small town in County Limerick in Ireland. In 1845, a potato disease spread through the country, killing crops and causing many people to starve. Now Seamus and his family have made the treacherous journey across the Atlantic Ocean to seek a new life in New York.

Flat cap

Torn, dirty clothes

Sack to carry belongings

Fiddle (violin)

Bodhrán (Irish drum)

Irish music

The Irish immigrants that moved to New York brought many traditions with them. They brought instruments so that they could play their traditional music in their new home.

▼ New York

Arriving into the port is a shock. There are lots of people and it is very dirty. Seamus and his family make their way to the Irish quarter of the city, where they rent a small, expensive space in a musty cellar.

Wagon carrying crates

Warehouses

Castle Clinton Immigration Station

New York cop

Family being reunited

Family carrying bags

Man wheeling cart

1845
During the Irish potato famine farmers struggled to grow crops and many people starved.

Potatoes

1847
Tens of thousands of immigrants leave Ireland and arrive in New York.

1860
A quarter of New York's population is now of Irish descent.

Shoes tied on with string

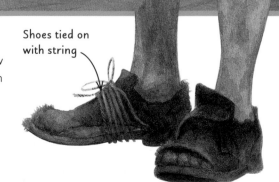

Risky journey

The journey from Ireland to the USA across the Atlantic Ocean was a dangerous one. The ships were often nicknamed "coffin ships" because they were unsafe and living conditions were very poor.

County Limerick

New York

Working on the tracks

Seamus and his father work hard every day laying railway tracks for the steam trains of the USA. His mother works in the city as a maid.

Tall rigging and large sails were used to catch the wind on the long voyage from Ireland to the USA.

Ships constantly dock with new arrivals.

Sailor climbing the rigging

Dock workers

Moving a heavy trunk

Tired after the long journey

New arrivals

1861–1865

Many Irish immigrants fight in the American Civil War.

Ellis Island Immigration Station

1892

Ellis Island becomes a centre where immigrants are checked on arrival in the city.

1961

John F. Kennedy, a descendant of Irish immigrants, becomes president of the USA.

President John F. Kennedy

The American Civil War

NORTH AND SOUTH USA DIVIDED

In 1861, war broke out between the northern states of the United States of America, the Union, and the southern states, the Confederacy. The two sides disagreed over the issue of slavery and whether the nation should stay united. Many died before the Union won the war in 1865.

Attack on Fort Sumter

On 12 April 1861, Confederate troops fired cannons at Union troops at Fort Sumter in South Carolina, starting the Civil War. The Union troops fired back, but were forced to leave the fort.

Freedom from slavery

Susie Baker King Taylor was born into slavery in 1848. Aged seven, she attended school in secret when staying with her grandmother. In 1862, aged 14, she fled with her uncle's family to Union-occupied land. She was given books to set up a school for children and adults.

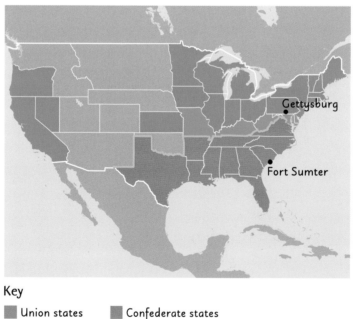

Gettysburg

Fort Sumter

A nation divided

People in the southern states of America mainly grew crops. Many slaves worked on the land, and were treated by their owners as possessions. People in the northern states were making goods in factories and had fewer slaves. Most of the fighting happened along the boundary between the two areas.

Key

- Union states
- Border states
- Confederate states
- Union/Confederate boundary

November 1860
Abraham Lincoln is elected president of the USA.

February 1861
Southern states form the Confederacy and elect their own president, Jefferson Davis, in November.

12 April 1861
The first exchange of fire takes place at Fort Sumter.

Union soldier cap

21 July 1861
First Battle of Bull Run is first major battle of the war.

Child soldiers

Although the youngest age for soldiers was officially 18 years old, younger boys joined up as drummers and messengers. Many were wounded or killed on the battlefield.

Drums were used to signal instructions to troops on the battlefield.

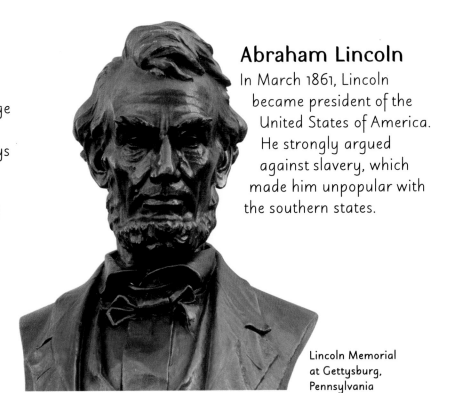

Abraham Lincoln

In March 1861, Lincoln became president of the United States of America. He strongly argued against slavery, which made him unpopular with the southern states.

Lincoln Memorial at Gettysburg, Pennsylvania

The end of the war

After the war ended in 1865, the states remained united and slavery was abolished. All children were given the right to education, although there were separate schools for black and white children.

17 July 1862
The Union approves the recruitment of black troops into the army.

Musket

1–3 July 1863
Battle of Gettysburg is won by the Union, but both sides are tired out.

9 April 1865
Confederates surrender, bringing the war to an end.

Anastasia

⭐ Real life

RUSSIAN PRINCESS AT THE TIME OF THE REVOLUTION

Grand Duchess Anastasia (1901–1918) was the youngest daughter of Nicholas II, the last tsar (emperor) of Russia. She grew up surrounded by wealth and privilege, enjoying the most beautiful clothes and regular visits to the ballet and theatre. However, her life was turned upside down when the revolution of 1917 ended her father's reign. The revolutionaries imprisoned Anastasia's family, later killing them all.

"It rains every day, but we still have breakfast and tea in the balcony..."
Anastasia's diary, 27 May 1916

Royal family

Anastasia had three elder sisters and one younger brother. Although they had many servants, while at home they slept on hard beds and were expected to tidy their own rooms.

Maria Alexandra Anastasia Tatiana Alexei Olga Nicholas II

Rich and poor

There was a huge gap between the rich and the poor in Russia. The tsar and upper classes could enjoy expensive objects, such as those made by court jeweller Carl Fabergé, while many poor people did not have enough food to survive.

Russian Revolution

Opponents of the tsar wanted to end his power and improve the lives of the poor. In 1917 they staged a revolution, sweeping away the royal family and killing their aristocratic supporters.

RUSSIA

St. Petersburg

Empire and palaces

The tsars had many palaces in their vast empire, but the favourite of Nicholas and his children was the Alexander Palace. It was built in the 1790s for Empress Catherine the Great at Tsarskoe Selo near the capital, St Petersburg.

1894
Nicholas II is crowned tsar of Russia.

Nicholas II at his coronation

18 June 1901
Grand Duchess Anastasia Nikolaevna is born near St Petersburg.

February 1917
The family is placed under house arrest in the Alexander Palace, Tsarskoe Selo.

15 March 1917
Tsar Nicholas gives up the throne.

August 1917
Revolutionaries move the family to Siberia, away from their supporters.

Princess in trouble

During the revolution, Anastasia and the rest of the family were imprisoned. They hid jewels and money inside their clothes and hoped to be rescued, but were killed in July 1918.

April 1918
The family is moved west of the Ural Mountains to Yekaterinburg.

17 July 1918
Anastasia and the rest of the family are secretly killed by revolutionaries in Yekaterinburg.

1920s
An impostor claims that she is Anastasia, and has survived the revolution.

Anna Anderson, the imposter

1922
Russia joins the Soviet Union, where many states formed to be one country.

2009
DNA tests prove that Anastasia and her family were killed in 1918.

World War I

FAMILY LIFE CHANGES WHILE THE WORLD IS AT WAR

Between 1914 and 1918, 30 countries around the world went to war, involving 65 million soldiers. Everyone in these countries was affected, with fathers and older brothers going to war, mothers going to work, and homes destroyed. Around 16 million people died and borders of countries changed as empires collapsed.

Call to action

Countries' leaders set up campaigns to encourage men to join the army and women to work, growing food and making weapons.

Campaign poster encouraging women to work

Poster telling people to grow their own food

Key

■ Neutral countries ■ Central Powers ■ Allied Powers

World at war

Many of the countries of the world took sides when Austria-Hungary invaded Serbia. The two sides were called the Central Powers (which included the German, Austro-Hungarian, and the Ottoman Empires), and the Allied Powers (which included the French, Russian, and the British Empires). Some countries did not join either side and remained neutral.

Into battle

A lot of the fighting in Europe took place along a line of trenches. Soldiers lived in these dirty, often flooded, ditches, and had to fight in the land between them. Many children lost their fathers in the battles.

28 June 1914
Archduke Franz Ferdinand of Austria is assassinated, prompting Austria-Hungary to declare war on Serbia in July.

August 1914
German troops cross through Belgium and invade France.

German gun called a howitzer

25 April 1915
Allied troops land on the Gallipoli peninsula in Ottoman Turkey.

The USA joins the war

In the summer of 1917, the USA sent soldiers to fight in Europe with the Allied Powers. This gave the Allies hope, and helped lead to their victory in November.

Children go to work

Many adults were dying in the fighting or from other causes, such as the Spanish flu. Hundreds of thousands of children had to leave school at 12, or even younger, and go to work in factories and on farms.

Signatures on the Treaty of Versailles

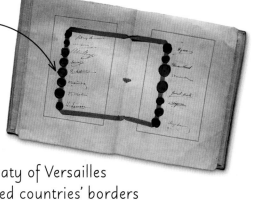

Peace at last

In November 1918, the Central Powers surrendered and fighting stopped. On 28 June 1919, the Treaty of Versailles was signed. It changed countries' borders and forced Germany to disarm and pay for much of the damage caused by the war.

Ambulance used on battlefield

1 July 1916
Battle of the Somme begins. More than one million troops die or are wounded in this battle.

6 April 1917
USA declares war on Germany.

11 November 1918
Fighting stops as an armistice, or truce, is agreed by both sides.

Hiren

CHILD WITNESSING GANDHI'S SALT MARCH

Hiren is a ten-year-old boy growing up in India in 1930. He loves going to school and his favourite subject is maths. His father grows cotton and, like most other people in their village, campaigns for Indian independence from the British. His mother supports the freedom movement by weaving cloth from cotton spun at home using the *charkha*, a type of spinning wheel. By doing this, the family doesn't need to buy British machine-made cloth.

Daily meals

Hiren's family does not eat meat. Their meals usually include *jowar* or *bajra* (types of grain), *rotlo* (flat bread), and pickled mango with *papad* (crackers).

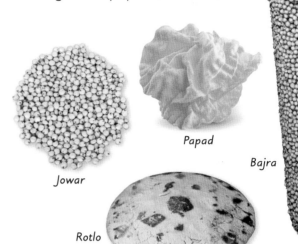

Jowar

Papad

Bajra

Rotlo

Gandhi

One of the most important leaders of the freedom movement is Mohandas K. Gandhi. He never uses violence in his protests and the villagers respect him deeply. They call him *Bapu*, which means "father" in Gujarati, the language spoken in this region.

▼ Salt March

The British charge money to produce salt, which many poor people cannot afford. Gandhi is leading a 386-km (240-mile) march from Sabarmati to the coastal village of Dandi to produce salt freely from seawater.

Village leader

Participants in the Salt March

Cotton being cultivated

Gandhi

People joining the march as it passes through their village

Fetching firewood

1857
First large-scale Indian rebellion organized by local soldiers against the British.

1885
Indian National Congress is founded to give Indians a greater voice in politics.

1905
Indians boycott British products under the Swadeshi movement.

1917
Gandhi protests against the forced farming of plants that provide indigo dye.

Spinning wheel

1921
Pingali Venkayya designs a new Indian flag with a *charkha* spinning wheel in the centre.

Gandhi cap

Shirt made of
homespun fabric

Cloth satchel
for carrying
school books

Rough-cut
leather
shoes

Where Hiren lives

Hiren's home is in Buva, a village in
the Gujarat province. Temperatures
can reach up to 45°C (110°F) in the
summer. He and his friends wait
for the monsoons when the rain
pours down and they can splash
in the puddles.

Buva

Stick games

Hiren plays board games
like snakes and ladders.
He also likes to play
gilli-danda, where a large
wooden stick called a
danda is used to hit a
smaller one called a *gilli*.
It is similar to the game
of cricket.

House with
corrugated
iron roof

Village
blacksmith

Mango
tree

Running to see
the march

Drawing water
from the well

Spinning
yarn

1930
Gandhi leads the
symbolic Salt
March to rebel
against the British.

1942
Gandhi begins the Quit
India Movement, a civil
disobedience movement to
put an end to British rule.

Jawaharlal Nehru

1947
India gains independence
on 15 August. Jawaharlal
Nehru becomes the first
Prime Minister of
Independent India.

World War II

WAR BREAKS OUT AROUND THE WORLD AGAIN

In 1939, Germany, led by Adolf Hitler, started to invade neighbouring countries. Fighting broke out across the world as countries took sides. Some countries such as Italy and Japan joined Germany and were called the Axis Powers. The opposing Allied Powers included Britain, the USSR, and later the USA. Children around the world were caught up in the conflict.

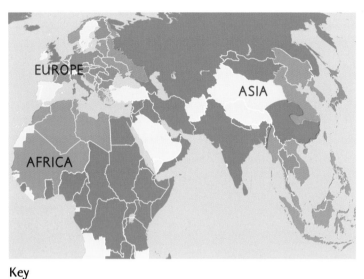

EUROPE
ASIA
AFRICA

Key
■ Allied Powers ■ Axis Powers ■ Countries controlled by the Axis Powers

Global conflict
Germany invaded countries in Europe to the north, east, and west. Fighting also spread across North Africa, Southeast Asia, and in the Pacific Ocean.

Nazi Party
Hitler led Germany's National Socialist, or Nazi Party, which held the view that certain races were better than others. German children were encouraged to join the Hitler Youth movement, and taught to follow Hitler and hate the Jews.

The swastika was the symbol of the Nazi Party.

Concentration camps
Jews and Roma gypsies were rounded up by the Nazis and taken to concentration camps. Children became separated from their parents, and millions of adults and children died in the camps.

September 1939
Germany invades Poland. War is declared on Germany.

German helmet

27 May 1940
Defeated Allied forces withdraw from France at Dunkirk.

British Lancaster bomber

September 1940
Battle of Britain between British and German air forces begins.

The USA joins the war

On 7 December 1941, Japan, one of the Axis Powers, bombed the US naval base at Pearl Harbor, Hawaii. The USA entered the war, joining and strengthening the Allied Powers.

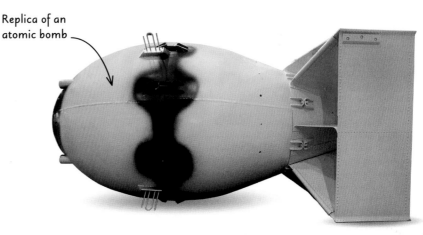

Replica of an atomic bomb

Lightning war

The German term *blitzkrieg* (lightning war) was used to describe the bombings of cities across Europe. Adults and children gathered in shelters during these air raids.

Atomic bomb

After Germany surrendered in May 1945, the USA wanted to force Japan to stop fighting, too. Atomic bombs were dropped on the Japanese cities of Hiroshima and Nagasaki in August, killing more than 135,000 people.

2 February 1943

Battle of Stalingrad ends, forcing Germany to withdraw from Russia.

German Tiger tank

6 June 1944

On D-Day, Allied troops successfully land on the beaches in France.

7 May 1945

Germany surrenders and war ends in Europe.

2 September 1945

Japan surrenders and World War II ends.

Susan

CHILD EVACUATED IN WORLD WAR II

Susan is a ten-year-old girl from East London. In September 1939, she and other children from her school are sent to a village on the edge of the Cotswolds in western England, to escape the danger of enemy bombing. Susan moves in with a family of strangers, goes to a new school, and discovers a different kind of life in the countryside.

Escaping the Blitz

The Germans' heavy bombing of Britain's big cities, factories, and docks begins in 1940. It is called the Blitz, which means "lightning" in German. Children evacuated to the countryside between 1939 and 1940 escape the worst of the bombing.

Label shows personal details

Box containing gas mask

Bag of belongings

Hay wagon

Buses drive children from the railway station.

Horses for transportation

Railway station

Sheepdog and sheep

Milkman

Suitcase containing clothes

1 September 1939
War is declared. The first evacuations begin.

Newspaper announcing the start of the war

January 1940
When bombing does not start, many evacuees return home.

June 1940
Bombings are again expected, and further evacuations happen.

Farmyard animals

The countryside is completely different from a big city. Most people in the countryside work on farms. Susan sees animals such as pigs, sheep, and cows for the first time in her life, and finds out how fruit and vegetables grow.

Rationing

Supplies coming to Britain are cut off by the German navy so most food, from meat to sugar, is rationed. From 1942 onwards, Susan is allowed just 200g (7oz) of sweets each week.

The journey

Susan travels by train from London to the Cotswolds, but evacuees also come from Britain's other big cities. They travel to villages in western England and Wales.

The Cotswolds

London

Keeping safe

Because poisonous gas was used in World War I, the government orders everyone to carry a gas mask at all times. The gas attacks do not come, but people are still fined if they are not carrying a mask.

▼ Arriving in the countryside

Susan and other children from her school arrive in the village in the countryside. They are told to stand in line while local people select the child they would like to look after.

Aeroplanes from a nearby airbase

Trains are powered by steam engines.

Village hall

Grocer's delivery van

Village church

Village shop

Postman

Delivery boy

Evacuees

Host families

September 1940 to May 1941
The Blitz causes massive damage to British cities.

June 1944
V-weapons (rockets and flying bombs) lead to more evacuations.

V-1 flying bomb used by Germany

8 May 1945
VE Day marks the end of the war in Europe.

June 1945
Officials allow children to return home.

Anne Frank

GIRL IN HIDING DURING WORLD WAR II

Anne Frank was a Jewish girl living in Amsterdam during World War II. When Anne was 11, Nazi Germany invaded the Netherlands and began sending Jews to concentration camps. Anne and her family went into hiding. She did not survive the war, but her diary was saved and has been published worldwide.

Amsterdam

Unsafe for Jews

The Nazis made Jews wear the Star of David badge and sent them to forced labour camps. Otto Frank, Anne's father, decided to put his family into hiding in the hope they would be safe from the camps.

Nazi invasion

The Nazis targeted Jews both in Germany and in the countries they invaded. This included the Netherlands, where Anne lived with her family in the capital city, Amsterdam.

The hiding place

The family moved into secret rooms in the building that housed Otto's office. The entrance was hidden by a bookcase, and only a few people knew they were there.

Anne's diary

Anne was given a notebook for her 13th birthday in June 1942. In it, she describes life in hiding and how she got on with her family.

> "I can shake off everything as I write; my sorrows disappear, my courage is reborn."
>
> *Anne's diary*

1929
Annelies (Anne) Frank is born in Frankfurt, Germany.

1933
The family moves to Amsterdam, hoping to avoid Nazi persecution.

Anne with her parents and older sister, Margot

1939
Germany invades Poland, and World War II begins.

May 1940
The Germans invade the Netherlands and begin targeting Dutch Jews.

5 July 1942
Anne's sister, Margot, receives a letter calling her to a labour camp.

The author
Anne wrote about wanting to be a journalist one day, but in 1944 the family was found and taken to concentration camps. Only Anne's father survived the war.

6 July 1942
Otto and Edith Frank and their two daughters go into hiding.

Nazi insignia from a train that took people to the camps

1944
The family is found and sent to different concentration camps.

1945
Anne dies in the Bergen-Belsen camp.

25 June 1947
Anne's diary is published for the first time.

The Cold War

COMMUNISM VERSUS CAPITALISM

Between 1947 and 1989, there were political and military tensions between countries that believed in two opposite ways of life: communism and capitalism. This tension was called the Cold War. Children were taught to be prepared for an attack from the other side.

In the USSR, children aged 10 to 15 went to summer camps that promoted communist beliefs.

Communism

Communist governments believed in sharing out everything between the people. Children were encouraged to tell the authorities if their parents disagreed with the government.

Capitalism

Capitalist governments encouraged people to own things and provide for themselves. The US government spied on people they suspected of holding communist beliefs.

US Senator Joseph McCarthy wanted to "clean" the USA of communism.

Different sides

Two of the world's largest countries, the USSR and China, had communist governments. They protected other communist countries. The USA was the most powerful capitalist country.

1945
World War II ends. USSR is the main power in Eastern Europe.

1949
NATO, a military alliance between North America and Western Europe, is formed.

1955
Warsaw Pact between Eastern European communist nations is agreed.

USSR's Sputnik I, the world's first artificial satellite

1957
USSR and USA start competing to see who can be the first to send spacecraft and people into space.

Vietnam War

In 1954, a long war in Vietnam, Southeast Asia, began. The communists in the North were supported by the USSR and China, while the South was supported by the USA. The communists won in 1975.

The Berlin Wall

Europe was divided by the Cold War: the communist East and the capitalist West. A wall separated East from West in the German city of Berlin. Anyone escaping from the East was shot.

A barbed wire-covered, concrete wall divided East and West Berlin.

End of the Cold War

In 1989, protests, strikes, and elections in Central and Eastern European countries ended communist governments. Then the USSR broke up in 1991, and new countries were formed.

General strike in Czechoslovakia in 1989

October 1962
US navy blocks USSR ships from delivering missiles to Cuba in the Cuban Missile Crisis.

1968
Tanks from USSR stop the revolt in Czechoslovakia.

1975
Communists take over Saigon, ending the Vietnam War.

1989
Communism begins to collapse in Eastern Europe.

Communist symbol (hammer and sickle) on USSR emblem

Civil Rights

THE FIGHT FOR EQUALITY IN THE UNITED STATES

For much of the 20th century, African Americans in the USA faced harsh segregation. This meant they weren't allowed to use the same facilities as white people, including schools. They also suffered from discrimination (unfair treatment) and violence. The Civil Rights Movement aimed to change this with protests across the USA and political campaigns for equal treatment for everyone.

NAACP

The National Association for the Advancement of Colored People (NAACP) was formed in 1909. Many young people joined, and they fought for equality and against discrimination.

Key

▪ Alabama, Georgia, and Mississippi

Southern troubles

Before slavery ended in 1865, there were many black slaves in the southern states, including Alabama, Georgia, and Mississippi. The worst crimes took place in these states, where lynch mobs often hanged black people.

Ku Klux Klan

During the 20th century, an extreme group called the Ku Klux Klan (KKK) opposed the Civil Rights Movement and attacked African Americans. Members of the group burned black churches and schools, and terrorized the black community.

KKK uniform

1919
Black communities are attacked in numerous riots.

1955
Murder of black 14-year-old Emmet Till sparks outrage.

1955
Rosa Parks refuses to give her seat to a white person on a bus, sparking a bus boycott.

1950s bus

Ending segregation

Years of protesting and campaigning eventually led to changes in the law that banned segregation. In 1954, the Supreme Court ruled that segregation in schools was illegal. This Tennessee school is shown on the first day that black children were allowed to attend, in 1957. The Civil Rights Act of 1964 was the most important change to the law, and banned segregation in all public places and buildings.

Black Power salute at the 1968 Olympics

Martin Luther King Jr.

Martin Luther King Jr. was an important leader in the Civil Rights Movement. He encouraged non-violent protest and is best remembered for his Washington, D.C., speech in 1963, in which he used the repeated phrase, "I have a dream".

Black Power

The phrase "Black Power" is used to describe the ongoing struggle of black people. This includes pushing for equal rights, for political power, and for good jobs. People raise their fists in a salute to support Black Power.

1960
Protesters in the South stage sit-ins, refusing to move from buildings.

1965
Civil Rights campaigner Malcolm X is killed in New York City.

1965
Voting Rights Act makes it easier for southern blacks to vote in elections.

1968
Martin Luther King Jr. is killed. Riots and protests follow.

Statue of Martin Luther King Jr.

Ruby Bridges

CIVIL RIGHTS PIONEER

Ruby Bridges is an African American from New Orleans. When she was born, African Americans were treated like second-class citizens, with laws keeping them separate from white people. This was known as segregation, and meant that black and white children had to go to different schools. In 1960, Ruby was the first black child to go to a previously all-white school. She grew up to be a civil rights campaigner.

New Orleans

The South

New Orleans, Louisiana, is in the south of the USA. Prejudice against African Americans was especially strong in the South, where most slaves lived before slavery was made illegal in 1865.

Segregation

The segregation policy kept races separate. There were different schools, restaurants, transport, and even public toilets for African Americans and white people. Most African Americans lived in poverty.

Protesters against equal rights marching with signs

Civil Rights Movement

In 1955, five years before Ruby went to her new school, Rosa Parks (right) refused to give up her seat on the bus for a white person. Protests against segregation such as this led to the Civil Rights Act of 1964, which banned discrimination based on race, colour, religion, sex, or national origin.

"The only tired I was, was tired of giving in."

Rosa Parks, activist

Protesters

Many white people, especially in the South, opposed moves to give equal rights to African Americans. They protested strongly against the new laws and many African Americans were the victims of violence.

8 September 1954
Ruby Bridges is born in Tylertown, Mississippi.

1954
A new law forces all-white schools to admit African-American children.

Troops guarding students

1957
Troops protect nine black students from violence in Little Rock, Arkansas.

1960
Ruby passes an entrance test to go to a desegregated school.

The walk from school

When Ruby started her new school, there were protests and threats made against her and her family. She was protected by US Federal Marshals, who drove her to and from school.

14 November 1960
Ruby starts at her new school, William Frantz Elementary.

1964
The Civil Rights Act prohibits segregation and discrimination in public places.

1988
About 45 per cent of black students go to previously all-white schools.

1993
Ruby volunteers at her old school. She encourages parents to be active in their children's education.

1999
Ruby forms the Ruby Bridges Foundation, promoting "tolerance, respect, and appreciation of all differences".

2001
Ruby receives the Presidential Citizens Medal from President Bill Clinton.

Children of the future

HOW CHILDREN MAY LIVE IN THE YEARS AHEAD

It is hard to guess how children's lives will be different a few decades from now. The amazing technological changes already happening, in areas from medicine to food production, may give us clues. What do you think the future will look like?

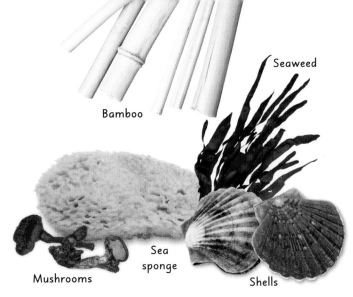

Bamboo

Seaweed

Mushrooms

Sea sponge

Shells

Earth-friendly buildings

The timber used to make buildings may one day run out. Future children may live in buildings made of other natural materials, like mushrooms and shells. Some people are already building using these materials.

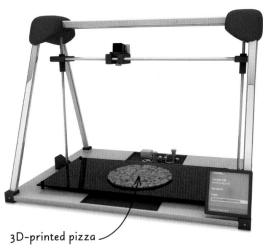

3D-printed pizza

3D-printed food

The US space agency NASA is working on 3D printing puréed ingredients that astronauts can eat on long missions to places such as Mars. One day children may eat 3D-printed pizza and biscuits, too.

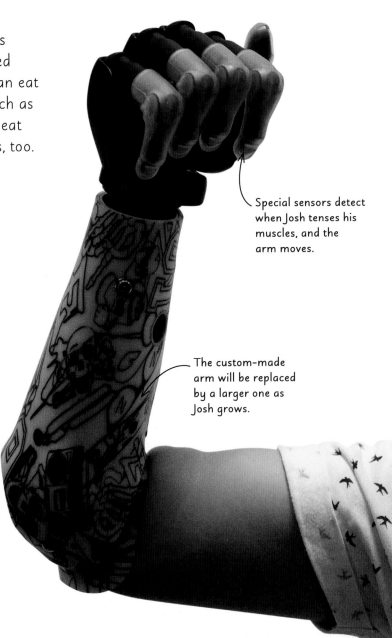

Special sensors detect when Josh tenses his muscles, and the arm moves.

The custom-made arm will be replaced by a larger one as Josh grows.

Sava is a Japanese robot programmed with six different facial expressions.

Artificial intelligence

Realistic robots are already being made for tasks like teaching school lessons. True artificial intelligence, with machines that can think for themselves, is probably a long way off.

Holidays in space

Companies are designing ships to take tourists into space. Some are even taking bookings! The first trips will be short, giving travellers an experience of a few minutes of weightlessness and a view of the curved surface of the Earth.

Mars

Earth

Nanotechnology

Robots no bigger than a blood cell may one day be able to fix health problems and attack diseases from inside our bodies. The science behind these robots is called nanotechnology.

Scientists are now developing bionic lungs and other internal body parts.

Bionic body parts

Nine-year-old Josh Cathcart from Scotland was born without a right hand. In 2015, he became the first child to get a bionic hand – an artificial hand that works like a natural one. Scientists are making other bionic parts that could act as "upgrades" to make people stronger or help them run faster.

Glossary

agriculture
Growing crops and raising livestock for food

Cows are used for milk and meat.

ally
Country that supports another country, and might agree trade deals or fight alongside them in a war

assassination
Murder of someone, usually a well-known person such as a politician or monarch

astronomy
Study of the Universe beyond the Earth, including space, solar systems, and galaxies

BCE
Abbreviation for "Before Common Era", which indicates dates earlier than the Common Era that began in year 1 and continue to the present

capitalism
Political or economic system where individuals own property and companies, instead of the government owning them

CE
Abbreviation for "Common Era", which indicates dates used from year 1 to the present

city-state
City that governs itself and is not part of any larger country or state

civil war
War fought between two opposing groups within one country or state

communism
Political or economic system where property, land, factories, and other facilities are owned by the government

crusades
Wars fought in the medieval period between western European Christian forces and Muslims from Turkey and the Middle East

Christians and Muslims clashing in the Second Crusade

dynasty
Family of rulers whose power passes from one generation to the next

empire
Group of countries ruled by a single monarch or government

famine
Extreme shortage of food, often caused by poor crop harvest

Irish immigrant

immigrant
Person who leaves their native country to settle in another country

independence
Freedom from outside control, such as when a country or area is no longer ruled by another country

merchant
Person whose work involves buying and selling large quantities of goods to make a profit

peasant
A poor person whose way of life is dependent on farming the land

pharaoh
Ruler of ancient Egypt

The death mask of the pharaoh Tutankhamun

pilgrim
Person who goes on a journey for a religious reason, usually to visit a holy place such as a shrine

Reformation
Movement in 16th-century Europe against corruptions in the Catholic Church that led to the formation of Protestant churches

Renaissance
A focus on art and learning in Europe that began in the 14th century, linked to a renewed interest in the ancient cultures of Greece and Rome

revolution
Sudden change that happens when a government or ruling power is overthrown, often quickly and by force

samurai
Japanese upper-class warriors that first appear in the medieval period

Samurai sword

scholar
Person who is an expert on a particular subject

segregation
Process of separating one group of people from another. For example, in the USA when African-Americans were kept separate from white Americans

slave
Person who is forced to work for or serve another person or family. Slaves are considered the property of their owners and forced to obey them

superpower
Country that has very great international power, and able to influence other countries.

The term was used especially to describe USA and the USSR in the decades after World War II

tax
Payments that have to be made by people or companies in a country to the government to fund various activities that the government pays for

Viking
Seafaring people from Scandinavia who raided, invaded, or settled in the coastal areas of northern Europe from the 8th to the 11th centuries

Viking ship

Index

Camera from the 19th century

Ancient Greek discus

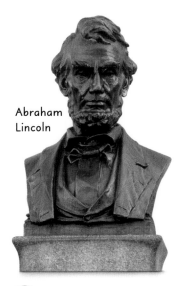

Abraham Lincoln

German helmet from World War II

Acknowledgements

DK would like to thank the following: Debangana Banerjee, Ishani Nandi, and Amina Youssef for editorial assistance; Syed Mohammad Farhan, Shipra Jain, Nityanand Kumar, and Mohd Rizwan for design assistance; Caroline Hunt for proofreading; Helen Peters for compiling the index; Ed Merritt for creating the maps; Jayati Sood for picture research; Rosie Adams and Dr Philip A. Clarke for their help with the Australian pages; Dr Diane Davies of mayaarchaeologist.co.uk for her help with the Maya pages; and James Dilley of AncientCraft for his help with the Ice Age pages.